Diana S. Gerson was educated at The American School for Girls in Baghdad and, after leaving Iraq, on a Kibbutz in Israel. She travelled to England where she trained as a nurse in Kent. She founded a successful Medical Employment Agency and is now retired. She has two children and six grandchildren, and lives in Bournemouth, Southern England.

OUT OF BAGHDAD

Diana S. Gerson

OUT OF BAGHDAD

Vanguard Press

VANGUARD PAPERBACK

© Copyright 2014
Diana S. Gerson

A CIP catalogue record for this title is
available from the British Library.

ISBN: 978 1 84386 755 5

*Vanguard Press is an imprint of
Pegasus Elliot MacKenzie Publishers Ltd.*
www.pegasuspublishers.com

First Published in 2014

**Vanguard Press
Sheraton House Castle Park
Cambridge England**

Cover concept: Sophia Molho

Printed & Bound in Great Britain

In memory of my dear husband, Gary Gerson, without whom I could not have completed this book.

Acknowledgements

My thanks to the staff at Pegasus Elliot Mackenzie Publishers for bringing this book to fruition. Thanks also to Dr Sophie Molho for the cover concept.

Introduction

In 587 B.C.E. Babylon and Egypt were in conflict over the lands at the Eastern end of the Mediterranean which contained Judah and its capital Jerusalem. A ruler of Babylon by the name of Nebuchadnezzar sacked Jerusalem and carried off into captivity in Babylon many influential Jews, large numbers of the Royal Family, nobles, landowners, military leaders, elders and priests[1] (see Notes on page 193). These Jews formed a Babylonian community which lasted for 2,500 years until the birth of the State of Israel. To the best of my knowledge, my ancestors came from these Jews who stayed in what was Mesopotamia and which is now Iraq, and did not return to the land of Israel. They were the first Jewish Diaspora and from the time of Mohammed lived under Moslem control.

The Iraqi Jewish community, particularly in Baghdad and Basra, prospered as a successful business and political entity which was needed by the government, but despite all this their status remained that of "Dhimmis", which was the term used for those subservient to Moslem rulers who could impose severe sanctions at any time they wished if Moslem laws were infringed by them in any way. They, like any other non-Moslem residents in a Moslem country, were only tolerated provided that they recognised the superiority of Moslem culture and religion. These Moslem laws were not however universally applied if there were sufficient advantages to the rulers in terms of financial or administrative benefits. There is no doubt that, overall, Jews prospered in Iraq over the 2,500 years, and in most cases were reluctant to leave the country even to return to Israel, despite the underlying threat of Mohammed's instructions to tolerate "The people of the Book", but to ensure that they obeyed Islamic law pertaining to non-Moslem residents such as Jews and Christians. This was to change for the worst in the last century when antagonism towards the Jews was augmented in the Second World War by Iraqi leaders supporting the Nazi regime, and also by pressure to establish a Jewish State. Zionism and Jews were equated and animosity towards the Jews evolved into open persecution. This culminated in the departure from Iraq of about 135,000 Jews after the foundation of the State of Israel. This was the background to my childhood years in Baghdad, most of which I was unaware of except for the increasing hostility before my departure.

Diana as a child in Baghdad

PART ONE

BAGHDAD

ONE

Early Memories

I was on the roof of our house when I first heard about Partition. I was ten years of age and living in Baghdad. When it was too hot at night and that was most of the summer, I slept on the roof along with my parents. Everyone that had a flat roof did the same. The evening breeze helped us to feel cooler. Minnie, my cat, would join me on the roof for the special treats that I brought for her and on the off-chance that a bird would land whilst she was on the look-out. There was no traffic down the "Street of the Trees", so called as both sides of the street were lined with eucalyptus trees. Each house had its individual architecture. Our house had a special basement room where we could keep cool at siesta time during the long hot summers. Apart from the laughter of my cousins next door and the distant noise from the open air cinemas, the twilight hours were quiet, but on that night my father said to my mother that things could get worse if the nations agreed on partition in Palestine. My father spoke several languages but he always spoke to my mother in Arabic for that was the only language she spoke. It was Arabic with a special dialect that the Jews in Iraq used but it was not accepted by the Arab population.

I understood what he meant by "things could get worse" because Jews in Iraq had to be cautious in everyday life as there was always a feeling of potential hostility from those we encountered in the street. I had heard about the troubles in Palestine and my friends and cousins would often discuss these matters. We all knew about incidents that had happened to Jews in recent times. Zionism was a bad word that was applied indiscriminately to all Jews. My cousin Yeheskel, who lived next door, arrived home one day after being severely beaten. He had inadvertently trodden on the boot of a soldier who was sprawled on the pavement. As soon as he apologised he was recognised as a Jew and received blows to his head and body. He was the oldest of my cousins who lived next door and we had never thought that he could come to any harm, although we knew that he and his friends were attending secret meetings of Zionist groups. Many Jews in Baghdad were affluent; there were quarters where the richer Jews lived and areas where the poorer Jews lived, although there was no ghetto. Life was pleasant for the wealthier Jews but none of them anticipated the way that they would be victimised following the establishment of the State of Israel. Interestingly, there was often a reversal of the fortunes of Jews, as those who arrived in Israel with very little found that they now had opportunities previously absent and prospered accordingly, provided that they were prepared to work hard.

We often talked about the stories of Jews who were hanged in public and the pogroms of 1941 labelled "The Farhud" where many Jews were murdered, although our parents tried to shield us from these stories.[2] Nonetheless, we all had Moslem Iraqi friends and life seemed to be going along happily for me with my many cousins.

TWO

American School

I attended The American School for Girls which was a private school. It was a Christian school but the pupils were a mixture of Moslems, Christians and Jews. There was a junior and senior school and every morning we sat in assembly for twenty minutes, at the end of which we were allowed to express our opinions if we wished. My cousins Doris and Daisy were at the same school. Walking to school with Doris was an ordeal as she always played tricks on me. One of them was to distract me by pointing at something excitedly, making me turn to look so that I walked into a lamp post. I fell for this several times. I much preferred to walk with Daisy who was older, more mature, sweet and gentle. She had her own friends and I suppose they wanted to talk about boys so I guessed that they didn't want me to tag along. I had no alternative but to walk with my tormentor.

My best friend was Huda and we sat together in class. She came to school in a chauffeur driven car and was a Moslem but we were always friendly. It was a beautiful school overlooking a big park and gardens. Some of the Moslem pupils would have their lunches brought to them by their butlers and they would eat them outside in the gardens. None of the Moslem girls in our school dressed in the traditional Arab clothing; far from it, they were very liberated and appeared every day in different designer outfits, as we did not have school uniform. Our school was like a fashion show at times. I was never interested in fashion so I found it rather boring as I felt school was for learning. In the streets of Baghdad few girls were covered up but were dressed in modern styles, but some of the older women wore the typical religious dress. There were no bars only night clubs and there were a few open air cafes where men drank their Arak and watched the passersby.

The Headmistress was American as were some of the teachers, the rest were mainly Iraqis. Our lessons were in English and Arabic and I had no problems in either language. I was preparing for the Baccalaureate and my teachers correctly forecast a good result for me. At school we would be taken for day trips and on one occasion we went to the site of the Hanging Gardens of Babylon, one of the ancient wonders of the world. The guide explained to us that Nebuchadnezzar had these gardens built to please his wife who came from Persia. She missed the greenery of her home town and he wanted to remind her of those beautiful landscapes. He used Jewish experts to design the gardens and his Jewish captives to build them.

Most Jewish children entered "Alliance" schools and a few girls went to the American school.[3] The children of families who could not afford these private schools went to the State schools. In these schools they were not treated as equals and had to be on their guard against any aggressive conduct from the other children.

Despite these problems, life seemed to run smoothly and people were contented in their own way. No one anticipated a sudden change in the very near future.

THREE

Family

I had four cousins, three girls and one boy, who lived next door, and we would play and read together. We would visit our uncles and aunts and other cousins and sometimes we were taken to the river bank for picnics. My memories of those days were happy ones; cooking a large fish on a spit by the Tigris River, going to parties at an uncle's house where he would hire a belly dancer and we girls would try to emulate her by wriggling and gyrating around the floor. Some of the best times were the Jewish holidays when we would gather at an uncle's house; there would be lots of children and we would laugh and sing together and we would have special foods. Before the Jewish New Year my parents and uncles and aunts would visit the graves of their ancestors. On this day, about fifteen children would gather at the house of Aunt Rosa, my father's sister. We were all excited and enjoyed the day chatting and playing until we were collected by our parents.

My father had three brothers and four sisters. One of his brothers died at an early age; apparently he was an excellent businessman, but he had a weak heart. He was very handsome and popular with women and his brothers were jealous of him. He had a childhood sweetheart but they were limited as to how much they could see each other, and needed to be chaperoned. A romantic aunt in the family sneaked them into her house one day and left them alone together for a few precious minutes. It seems that he kissed her hand for a prolonged few moments; he then closed his eyes and the girl tenderly kissed both his eyes. The aunt must have been watching from somewhere and that was the first and last time they kissed. My uncle passed away that week from a heart attack. My grandmother and the young girl were inconsolable. I am told that the girl stayed with my grandmother for a long time. When my aunt told that story she could not stop crying and whenever we recalled the story we wept too.

One of my father's sisters was called Mazal. Her husband was called David and he was a rich businessman from Basra. Mazal was a pretty and sweet natured girl and David adored her. She used to go from Basra to visit her family in Baghdad a few times each year. David missed her when she was away and the story goes that, on her return, he would have a band playing music for her and he would fill the house with flowers. One day, when all was ready as usual for her return, she did not appear. She had died suddenly due to a previously undiagnosed heart complaint, similar to that of her brother. Uncle David was broken hearted but remained with the family so that they could grieve together. Some years later, David married Mazal's sister Georgia. They had one still-born baby, and never had any more children but they had a long and happy marriage. My father had another brother who had anticipated the future difficulties for the Jews and he left Baghdad with his family to go to Palestine in the thirties. They must have missed Baghdad as they would come back for regular visits.

My mother had three sisters and three brothers, so we were not short of family for the various festivals. I, as an only child, felt as if I had many brothers and sisters by having so many cousins. We are now all scattered around the world but we never lost touch and we meet at many family occasions, especially weddings. The gatherings are usually large and we always enjoy them. Most of our families are in the U.S.A., Canada or Israel and despite the distances that separate us, we probably see each other more frequently than many people whose families are in the same country. On these occasions, Gary, my husband, and I try to combine the family visits with other events such as the theatre on Broadway or film festivals. Gary is very happy to visit my family with whom he has an excellent rapport.

At home in Baghdad, my mother had a woman who helped her in the house doing cleaning and odd jobs. She was a Moslem, very tall and always dressed from head to foot in black; we called her Um Agul. She had a daughter and son and they lived nearby in a shed-like dwelling. They also used our garage for their personal effects. The daughter married a jockey, the son also married and they all lived together. They were very kind and used to take me for walks. We were all very friendly but for Minnie, my cat, who hissed at Um Agul whenever their paths crossed.

My father worked for Iraqi Airways as an administrator. They had a close relationship with British Overseas Airways Corporation (B.O.A.C.) and my father's knowledge of English was an asset as some of the personnel were British. He had previously travelled to the East for the family business which was importing and exporting various commodities, and he had lived in Japan for some time. I was a toddler when he returned to Baghdad and we never really bonded because I resented his absence for so long. The family said that my father was not successful in that business and they did not forgive him as he was supposed to have promoted the business in his travels around the world. The business certainly suffered during this period but my father seemed to enjoy it. I think that he was not overly enamoured with the business and he knew that with his education he would always be able to get a good job. He returned to Baghdad via the United States and took up his position with Iraqi Airways. My headmistress had also lived in Japan and my father, when he met her on occasions, would talk to her in Japanese which impressed everybody around. I was upset when the headmistress asked me if I spoke any Japanese and if my mother and I enjoyed Japan. My answer was that we had not been there. A little silence followed; I think we were both uncomfortable with that question.

The interesting thing about my father was that although he was keen for me to be well educated and paid for an expensive private education, he seldom communicated with me or demonstrated any affection towards me apart from an occasional outing to the country. He did not even chastise me and though I sought his love, this rarely appeared and was probably the reason I became self-reliant. At times I would even try to antagonise him in order to achieve a response. He liked to rest in the afternoons, but I would beat my drums loudly to disturb him, but even this did not elicit a smack. He was afraid to have confrontations of any kind. My father claimed that an uncle of mine, my mother's brother, owed him money from a past transaction between them. On several tiresome occasions he sent my mother and I to visit my uncle to ask him for the money which he owed my father. My mother would not come into the house and face my uncle and I, who was only about 9 years old, had to go in and ask my uncle for the money. He was impressed with my confidence although, in fact, I did not need any additional confidence as I felt in control of the situation. I was able to deal with adults where they could not face each other, and to me it was a game in which I was a double agent! My uncle wanted to explain to me that he did not really owe my father anything anymore as far as he was concerned and this matter should be settled once and for all. He felt that it was not proper to send a little girl to deal with this business and that my father should have come himself. I explained that my parents were not able to deal with the matter at the moment, although I did agree with what he said. He reluctantly handed over the money and at the same time gave me a reward for being so understanding. When I got home I received another reward this time from my father when I informed him that I had defended his claim. It turned out to be a profitable day for me. I felt like the character in the film "The Go-between" from the classic story by L. P. Hartley. However, this story was not about love but rather an ugly dispute within a family as my uncle was also my father's cousin. Shortly after my last visit, my uncle and his family fled Baghdad. They left their very beautiful house and their possessions behind. They had several connections with business friends in Persia, as Iran was then called. With this, my yearly income suffered as there were no more transactions.

My father, in his capacity as a supervisor, would start work early and then return home at lunch time, eat a meal and then sleep in the basement in the afternoon where it was somewhat cooler. My father had a room upstairs which he kept locked and which I was forbidden to enter. My cousin Doris and I had often wondered what was in this room and why we were not supposed to find out. One day when Doris was at my house we found a key on a bookcase shelf. We guessed that it might belong to the locked door of the forbidden room and we decided to try it, although we knew that we should not. We were always adventurous and willing to try most things, and now curiosity overcame us. We checked that my father was asleep, and then we went upstairs and tried the key in the lock of the mysterious room. It turned, and we cautiously entered the rather dusty room. Looking around, the room seemed empty except for a small table and chair and a few suitcases on the floor. We put one of them on the table; it was not locked. We opened it and there was a collection of postcards from around the world. There was scenery and pictures of towns, places of interest and many pictures of women in their national dress. We were surprised to see some scantily dressed women holding fans in front of them, and some from Paris with balloons in front of them, as well as Japanese girls in kimonos. There was even an advertisement cut from a newspaper of a dance hall in New York with a price of a dime a dance with a hostess. It looked as if this collection of cards and pictures chronicled my father's journey around the world whilst promoting the family business. We looked through all the suitcases which also contained interesting souvenirs, and then we heard my father shouting to ask my mother if she had seen the key to his room. For a moment we froze, looking at each other in shock. Quickly we closed the suitcases, left the room and locked the door, but what to do with the key? We went down the stairs and dropped the key on the floor by the bookcase as we saw my father coming back from the kitchen. Doris said politely, "Hello uncle, how are you", we then went to the garden to discuss what had happened. Although our intrusion had been an adventure, I began to think about what kind of man my father was. He was certainly no businessman from what I understood, so his travelling around the world away from us for such a long time was simply for his own pleasure. I was angry and sad about this, not so much for myself as for my mother. She was blissfully ignorant of the material we had discovered I thought and it would have been cruel to expose her to the facts. Perhaps she did know some of this and chose not to acknowledge it. I decided that some things were better kept unspoken.

My father knew a private dentist by the name of Selim Guli who was an Armenian. I do not know how he knew him but he would send me on the bus to see him. I did not like him because he was abrupt and his dentistry painful. When I sat on the chair he would say, "How are you doing at school?" and I would say, "OK" and he would say, "OK is not good enough, private schools are very expensive." He would ask, "How is your father?" and in the same breath, "Open your mouth," before I had time to reply. He was short with large spectacles and his nurse was tall, young and good looking, and I could see that he was making eyes at her while probing in my mouth. She eyed me with suspicion and seemed to enjoy seeing me suffer under the drill. I did my best to make them feel uncomfortable by staring at them as if to say I know what is going on. I was glad to leave his surgery and I took his magazines from the waiting room on my way out as revenge. The dentist was a married man with grown up children and it did occur to me to blackmail them; I spent many hours fantasising about this idea. I called my cousins to meetings to discuss this idea and I promised to split any money gained, but after a while they refused to support me as they said no one would believe us. That was the end of my big money-making plan. He didn't look after my teeth properly and to this day I still have trouble with my teeth.

One thing about these dental visits that always puzzled me was that I never saw my father pay the dentist any money. I did once ask my father how the bills were settled and he just smiled. I did think that perhaps my father had some kind of hold over the dentist, the sort of thing that you see in the movies.

My mother was depressed for most of the time and probably from the time I was born, as I was told in later years. My parents never gave me presents such as toys, although I did have pocket money. My parents seemed to forget when I was born, although it was believed to be one day in April, so there were never any birthday parties. I never had to worry about naming a doll as I was never given one. I think that is why I always love to give things to children and see the happy expressions on their faces. This in some way made up for the lack of such gifts in my own childhood. I explained this to my grandchildren and they were upset and one of them gave me her teddy bear. My own happiness in those times came from reading. Throughout my life, books, movies and music have been very important to me. My father was away at the time I was born and my mother was not capable of knowing or remembering anything. She suffered a severe post-natal depression which was not readily diagnosed in those days. One doctor who she saw was sympathetic and sent her to Lebanon hoping that the new and beautiful environment would help her to recuperate. I was left behind with my aunt, and although I was happy I was bewildered as to where my mother had gone. I thought perhaps that there was something frightening about me which made her run away. I also wondered why there was no daddy, like my cousins had. This convinced me that there was something wrong with me. I even began to call my aunt's husband papa and demanded to be treated the same way as his daughters. He was a kind and easy going man and promised to do so. He was not educated so he had nothing in common with my father, therefore, the two of them never communicated. However, unlike my father, my uncle was full of love and caring.

I was named Souad which was an Arabic name and was thought to be more acceptable in an Arab world than a Jewish sounding name. Later I changed my name to Diana.

My parents were cousins. During the First World War men were conscripted into the Turkish Army in Iraq which, at that time, was part of the Ottoman Empire. My mother's brother and her father both went to war and both died, although the details of their deaths were not revealed. It was possible to pay to gain exemption from serving in the forces but my grandmother could not afford this and by the time she approached her wealthier brother, Joseph, who could have helped, it was too late, and they had both been sent away to fight for the Turkish Army. Joseph was compassionate and loved his sister dearly. He understood that she was a proud and shy lady but he wished that she had come to him earlier so that he could have helped her. He was well known in the community for his charitable works. I was told that people came to him seeking his wisdom and justice when they were troubled. I would like to think of him as a kind godfather. He was later to become my grandfather when his son married by mother. He was also a very good businessman. I never met him but I can imagine what he looked like, just as I try and imagine all my grandparents that I never knew (looking like movie stars!). My grandmother was pregnant at this time with my mother who therefore never knew her father or her brother. My grandmother was left with six children to bring up on her own. She even managed to send one of the boys to be educated. The girls went to sewing school from an early age. They were very happy and loved their mother very much. She was hard working and very protective of her children. One day there was a knock on her door and when she opened it there was a young man, nicely dressed standing on her doorstep. He asked her if that was the house of the Saul's. She said, "Yes" and asked him in. He said his name was Matook, and his trade was in cloths and tailoring. He and his father were commissioned to supply the army with uniforms. They had to measure the soldiers and that was how he met her husband, Saul, who had talked about his family, where they lived and how much he missed them every day. He said he could not wait to get back home and he hoped that it would be soon as he had a good, loyal and lóving wife fighting for his release. He was very eager to return to his lovely children. Matook had never forgotten that memory and the friendship he had made and decided that he would try and find out what had happened to his friend, Saul. My grandmother told him how hard she had tried to locate her husband. She had finally obtained the money for his release but by then he had been posted elsewhere. Her son had also been sent to an unknown location and she had spent many hours at the military offices searching for information. However, no one could help her and she was advised to go home and wait for news, which never came. She had her other children to look after and there were no more tears left to shed. Although the war had by now ended some time ago, the two men never returned. At this point, the girls came home from sewing school. As teenagers they were rather shy when they saw the stranger. He immediately liked my Aunt Georgia who seemed to welcome his attentions. My grandmother also liked him and he was invited to stay to dinner. He was very impressed with the way they presented their simple, but tasty, dishes on their limited income. There were no complaints connected with their company and it was the cheerful atmosphere in their humble house that he liked most of all. Subsequently he became a regular visitor. He understood that their financial situation was difficult and being a very generous man he brought many groceries with him every time he visited. He liked the happy atmosphere in the house and in time he asked for Aunt Georgia's hand in marriage. My grandmother and her siblings were delighted. Life had smiled on them and I acquired my lovely cousins and the man I came to call Papa. My grandmother died a few years later, before I was born. It was in fact at her funeral that my parents met. My father's parents died before I was born and so I never knew any grandparents. I would have loved to have had just one grandparent to love and be loved by. Even to this day, I feel that part of my life is missing. I have asked a lot of questions about them and I have heard nothing but praise for every one of them. My father's mother was a beautiful high society lady, gentle and charming and people talked about her charitable work. My maternal grandmother was, apparently, a saintly lady who had suffered much hardship losing her husband and a son, and nevertheless raised her remaining children with great devotion. Now that I am a grandmother, I feel blessed by having six lovely grandchildren whom I adore and am so lucky to be able to enjoy them.

My father had a sister called Farha. She lived in one of the poorer Jewish areas of Baghdad. She was pretty, a good cook and well organised. I loved to visit her. Her husband was an intelligent man who spoke three languages and was a highly qualified book-keeper with a great sense of humour. We had a kind of understanding between us which irritated his children who misunderstood him. He was unfortunately a gambler so that the family never had much money. Despite this, my uncle and aunt were very much in love and this made me feel happy when I saw them. She had four children, three girls and a boy. I was very friendly with them and visited them regularly. I would stay overnight at their house on many occasions and had great fun being with them. I never thought that I was imposing on them too much and my parents never advised me otherwise. I had the feeling that they liked me being away from home as they never objected or showed any signs of missing me. Many of my days I spent next door at my Aunt Georgia's. I think, at times, I hoped that they would object to my absence; that would have made me feel wanted especially when strangers used to make the comment that I was always at someone's house and didn't my parents miss me? I did not have an answer to that question so I would ignore it but it did hurt a lot. I did wish that one day they would come for me and ask me to come home as they missed me, but that never happened. Next door to my Aunt Farha lived a Moslem family who had a daughter aged sixteen whom I knew. One day my Aunt Farha told me the sad story of how this girl became pregnant and her fate. Aunt Farha was overlooking their garden from one of her bedrooms and heard the girl pleading with her brothers and some cousins not to kill her with knives but to use a gun. Apparently my aunt witnessed the men stabbing her to death. None of them was punished as it was considered an honour killing. The story upset me greatly and whenever I stayed with two of my cousins, Rachel and Georgette, in their room with a window overlooking the garden where the girl was stabbed to death, I would put the two cousins in the beds nearest the window and I would take the third bed nearest the door so that I could be furthest away from the scene of that crime and the fear associated with it. It always puzzled me that they never made any objection to my sleeping arrangements.

My mother had a sister named Lulu. She was fair with blue eyes and very pretty. One day, when she was fifteen, she caught the eye of a wealthy man who wanted to marry her and this was arranged. Lulu was very unhappy with her husband who was not treating her kindly, and his mother, who lived with them, was also very unpleasant towards her. She informed her mother and one day when her husband was not in the house my grandmother went and took Lulu away to her home. It was proved that her husband was abusive. Lulu never married again. Whether this was because the husband refused to give her a religious divorce, or for any other reason, I do not know but we all loved and cared for my Aunt Lulu. She used to take pleasure in telling us the story of how her dear mother rescued her from her evil husband and how a tiny woman like her mother stood up against a big burly man and his monster of a mother. They came knocking on the door demanding the return of Lulu. Poor Aunt Lulu went to hide shaking with fear. Her sisters comforted her, assuring her that no one would take her away. My grandmother stood her ground and told the husband that she would expose him in the community as she had a witness who had seen through a window in their house how he and his mother had been tormenting Lulu. Also, she would do her utmost to disgrace him in the Synagogue and things would be very unpleasant for him if he ever asked for Lulu again. My grandmother added that she had certain information about the mother's past; at that, the mother grabbed her son and said, "Let's go, she is not worth it." Apparently, at that point, my grandmother advanced towards the woman and for good measure pulled her hair saying, "That's what you used to do to my daughter." To the amusement of every one, the woman's hair came off in my grandmother's hand; it was a wig! It was a great pleasure to watch Aunt Lulu's face when she told the story and the story lengthened through the years. Aunt Lulu lived with her brother's family for a long time and acted as a nanny to his four children. Her older brother, Uncle Nissim, never held a proper job and at times Lulu and Nissim would stay at one of their sisters' homes. They were happy in their own way but they never had a home of their own. I always felt that this was sad but it did not seem so for them.

My cousin Yeheskel, the older brother of Daisy and Doris, was always difficult and had an evil sense of humour. On one occasion, when I was about nine years old, he challenged me to climb a tree in their garden. He said he would catch me if I jumped. I climbed the tree but when I jumped he did not even bother to attempt to catch me. Fortunately, I only suffered minor injuries, but I was very upset with the incident. I avoided Yeheskel for a long time after that, but I forgave him and still liked him for many years. It was perhaps because of this incident that I had some episodes of nightmares and sleep-walking; this was particularly worrying as I was sleeping on the roof because that was where the whole family slept during the hot summer nights in Baghdad. I used to try and count the stars in the sky when I lay in bed, and whilst counting them I would fall asleep. I suppose it was like counting sheep. My sleep-walking and nightmares got worse and one night I was found dangling from the rails of the roof. It was decided that I should be taken to see a Rabbi who had a reputation for helping with these problems and eradicating any evil factor involved. My mother could not face the mental stress of going with me, so her sister Aunt Georgia was delegated to accompany me. She was a believer in religious interventions in these matters. We duly arrived at the prayer hall attached to the Synagogue. It was a gloomy place with several men praying in low voices. I was brought before the healing Rabbi who was sitting cross-legged on a mat. I sat before him on the floor; he was a big man with crossed eyes which was very confusing to me as I thought that this might be connected with his healing power. There was a fly buzzing between us and he swatted it with a fly-swatter. I flinched and was disgusted. It was not a good start to our session. He stared intently at me whilst my aunt explained the problem; he then nodded and placed his hand on my head while saying some prayers. I can still remember his face which frightened me. I was relieved to get away and told my aunt that I didn't want to ever go back there again, and in fact, my nightmares and sleep-walking did stop, although I think it was more to do with me not wanting to return to see that Rabbi than the prayers that were spoken for me. I now developed insomnia and perhaps this was because I was frightened of my problems recurring if I fell asleep. To this day, I am frightened of the dark and sleep with the light on and read to all hours.

About this time I developed pneumonia. I was very ill and I thought the end was near. I asked for Doris, my cousin, to be brought from school so that I could say goodbye to her. We were about the same age and very close. She was the leader in our friendship, as I was not as quick-witted as her. Then I had a dream about my grandmother, Miriam. I had never met her but had heard many lovely stories about her and had seen her photographs. She arrived in a carriage and asked to take me away. I had a strange feeling as if floating on a cloud and being happy to see her; I tried to tell her to wait for me so that I could go with her yet I could not move. My mother held out her arms and refused to let me go. My grandmother said she could wait no longer and departed. I recovered but I still remember that dream in detail. It seemed like my time was not yet up so heaven can wait.

Uncle Sassoon, my father's brother, figured a lot in my life. When he married Marcelle, who came from a rich family, I was a bridesmaid and one of her younger brothers, Nori, was a page boy at the wedding and we became childhood friends. It is a pleasant feeling to maintain a relationship with past friends.

After losing touch with one another, Nori and I were to meet many years later in Montreal, his home town, at a family function. It was strange that now we were both grandparents, he declared his undying love for me, however, I could not recall that we were in love! I would say we were fond of each other. He was one of seven boys and one girl, his sister, Marcelle. His eldest brother was a very rich man and he used to have great parties in the happy days of Baghdad. My mother and I would be collected in a chauffeur driven car which took us to their family country home. It seemed strange to me that my father was never included. I enjoyed those parties greatly and Nori and I had fun together. As we grew up, we went in different directions and lost touch until we met again after several decades. He has remained a good friend and whenever my husband and I are in Montreal he collects us from our hotel and drives us everywhere.

Uncle Sassoon and Aunt Marcelle were to have two daughters and a son. Myrna was their eldest daughter and she was a good deal younger than me, but we were very close and we still see each other frequently, although she now lives in the United States. After medical studies in Israel and Canada, she became a successful Dermatologist. Her sister, Judy, was a lovable baby. She became a teacher in Montreal, and their brother, Joe, was the baby of the family whom I loved and spoiled. He was to become an orthopaedic surgeon in Florida, and we still all manage to meet at family celebrations.

My mother had a cousin called Selim who lived with his parents and sister in a poor village in the countryside outside Baghdad, near the Euphrates River. The interior of his house was well furnished and decorated but the area around it was impoverished. The locals tended to be uneducated. Sometimes my mother used to take me there to spend the day. Before I left for this trip I would always give Minnie, my cat, her breakfast. I would try and feed her with a boiled egg which was what Um Agul, our helper, suggested. Poor Minnie tried to eat it but she did not seem to enjoy this food. I found out in later years that cats don't eat boiled eggs! Going to the country seemed to relieve my mother from her depressed state. We always had fish fresh from the river at our cousin's home. My cousin Selim worked at the Ottoman Bank in the city and commuted there by bus. I looked forward to his return from work as he always made me laugh. He was well educated and in his early twenties. He was slim and athletic and adored by his parents. He would tell me about his experiences at work that day. One day we ventured outside the house; the outlook was not very pleasant, there were many people sitting on mats outside their houses. We were about to return indoors when my cousin suddenly sang a song about the beautiful nights of Vienna with all their glory. The description bore no relationship to what we were seeing in front of us. I burst out laughing and the more I laughed the louder he sang. Suddenly we both froze as we realised the people sitting down were not amused. They all stood and approached us menacingly. We entered the house quickly. There was banging at the door and shouts of "Zionist spies". They had never heard of Vienna and had decided that it was some sort of coded message. There was a decent man amongst the crowd who understood and managed to explain that it was only a song and calmed the locals down. Selim's parents had been very frightened about the incident fearing that their son would be taken to prison. I still think it was all very funny, although of course it was scary. I was always glad to get back home. I did not like the area or the people there and apart from the books and movie magazines that my mother gave me, I found the day trip boring. I did not object to going as I knew that my mother would be upset. These trips meant a lot to her and she was at her happiest when she was with a crowd of cheerful people. She could be good company and people liked having her around but I noticed that whenever there were noisy children around she would become agitated as if they were going to harm her. I realised that she did not enjoy the company of children. I would have liked to explain to her that her attitude was not a correct one but I never did.

Another cousin named Moshe, the Hebrew name for Moses, who I still see at family functions, lives in Israel. He is the son of my father's sister Rosa. In Baghdad, Moshe was an unfortunate name to have in our times. He would immediately be known as a Jew and taunting and bullying would follow this recognition. This would happen in certain areas. We were all fond of my Aunt Rosa who had three children. The eldest, Abraham, was kind and liked to entertain me and my mother with the stories of all the latest movies he had seen. My Uncle Sassoon lived at Aunt Rosa's for a while when he was a bachelor. His sister loved him and spoiled him with all sorts of treats. He would hide some of them for me whenever he knew I was coming round. It was our secret and I loved sneaking into his room to find the treasures which he had hidden away for me. I looked forward to these visits and I keep a good memory of Aunt Rosa. I never saw her get angry or complain. She was a woman of few words with an agreeable nature and lovely smile. Sometimes I compared my mother unfavourably with her.

It was a common practice when my family and friends were gathered together, that we would exchange stories about the history of the Jews in Baghdad. Frequently we would talk about our origins and way of life. King Nebuchadnezzar and his relationship with our people was a popular topic. He had been kind to the Jews and had respected them despite the fact that he marched them all the way from Jerusalem to Babylon. I suppose he thought that a nice long walk in the hot sunshine would not harm them! Once they arrived at the rivers of Babylon and were settled, he realised how valuable they were to his kingdom. Other tales concerned King Harun Al-Rashid. The story goes that this King's illnesses were always cured by the chicken soup that was prepared by his Jewish chef and she was soon appointed his head chef. Some said that he was very good to the Jews who were constant visitors to his palace. He thought highly of their wisdom especially in financial matters. He also trusted their doctors who proved to be excellent at their work and many of them were entertained at the lavish banquets he gave. When I heard such stories I would ask, with excitement, how many belly dancers were present. This would irritate the others who were telling stories. I suppose that because I did not receive much attention at home, I often escaped into a world of fantasy and enjoyed not only making up a story but relating it to family and friends. I would dream that I was Scheherazade and was summoned to tell stories to the Caliph of Baghdad who suffered from insomnia. I became so engrossed with my fantasy that one day I decided to share my own dream and I informed as many young cousins of mine as I could that I had something exciting to tell them. I told them all to gather at my house to meet in secret. To my surprise, thirteen of them arrived. They all sat around waiting for me to begin my secret story. I felt like Sinbad, the sailor, telling a crowd about his adventures at sea. They were all becoming impatient and eager for me to commence. I started by passing some sweets around that I knew everybody liked. It was a good move of mine since they all started to relax as they ate their sweets. I needed time to gather my thoughts about how I should begin. I started by enquiring if they had all heard of

King Harun Al-Rashid and how kind he had been to the Jews. Most of them nodded so I knew that they had some historical knowledge. I took a deep breath and continued slowly; one day the King became bored with all the cakes and desserts he was given and, as he was going to give a large banquet, he wanted something new and special for a dessert. A very pretty young Jewish girl heard about the King's problem. She told her parents that she would like to make some little cakes for the King's birthday. She promised they would be delicious for it was her own recipe. She called them Baklava. She sent them to the King and there was a delighted expression on his face when he tried one. He just could not have enough of them and requested to meet the girl who had made them. Once he saw her, and how pretty she was, he said that he would like to make her one of his wives (as he was allowed to have four wives), but he was told that she was Jewish. He decided to grant her a wish. The wish was that the community be allowed to build a new synagogue. That was how our great synagogue was built and how Baklava has been popular ever since. I finished my story by asking the cousins if they had guessed who this woman was. They shook their heads indicating that they did not know. I informed them that it was our great, great, great grandmother. Their faces expressed some doubt and there was no applause. I must say that to this day I still have a hard time getting the cousins to be convinced about any of my stories, even if they are true. I do have a long history of exaggerating (a little).

I have some memories of my childhood and being short of pocket money. I would try to think of ways to improve my finances. I had to devise a clever plan to target the right person at the right time and this was not an easy task. I finally came up with the right solution and proceeded to carry out my plan. I would visit two of my aunts and I knew that they did not like to be told that they looked well. They preferred that people would feel sorry for them. I would listen to their complaints and how hard their domestic chores were for them. Their husbands and children did not understand how hard it was to run a house, and did not seem to be able to be good listeners about any complaints they made. I would wait till their families were around them and then say that I was worried at how tired and pale the aunties looked. They certainly needed attention. They would all turn around and look at them and they were puzzled by what I was saying. I managed to make them feel uncomfortable although, in fact, the aunts would look very healthy. My aunts would look very pleased with my wise pronouncements. I had achieved my goal and I would then say goodbye and head for the door followed by an aunt who would thrust some pocket money in my hand. She would also compliment me and say how nice it was to have such a feeling niece and to visit her again soon. It was not easy to earn one's money; it needed a lot of guile and good acting to perform such a task. Pretending is rather hard work. There was a third aunt who had a different view of her wellbeing and was not so difficult to approach. I merely had to tell her how beautiful and young she looked and that it was a pleasure to have her as an aunt. The pocket money that resulted was usually more if the room was full of people. Her husband usually looked at me very suspiciously which made me very uncomfortable. As I said a quick goodbye, he winked at me with a smile as if we were sharing a secret.

I sometimes wonder whether I should feel guilty about the psychological ploys that I used in order to extract money from my unsuspecting aunts. But I soon forget these thoughts, and any regrets are overcome by my amusement at the memories.

FOUR

Political Background

It was towards the end of 1947, some weeks after I first heard about Partition that our lives changed dramatically. It was announced that the United Nations had voted in favour of the separation of Palestine into two states. We heard that both America, under President Truman, and Russia supported Partition.[4] We knew that this meant there would be a legitimate home for Jews. That day my father brought home chocolates and sweet treats in order to celebrate and this was certainly a rare event. However, that evening we all stayed indoors as we could not be seen celebrating in the street when Iraqis were all angry at the decision. My father said that now that the British would no longer have the mandate for Palestine, Jews would be allowed to enter freely. However, there was a problem for Jews living in Arab countries. Their departure would depend on whether the country would let them sell their houses, and if they could take their possessions with them. The next day at school conversation and chatter were subdued. Between lessons the Jewish girls stayed together and whispered about the news. One of the American teachers said that it was a good thing for people to have their own home. This teacher who was much liked by the pupils found that rumours began to spread that she was pro-Zionist. She was no longer popular and it was common knowledge that she was being investigated in case she was a spy, which of course she was not, she was not even Jewish. Soon after, it was announced at the assembly that she was returning to the United States for family reasons. That was the last we saw of our lovely teacher. We were asked to write essays with our own choice of subject. My story involved a thief, in the style of Robin Hood, inspired by a book I had been reading. It was actually several books about a famous gentleman-thief in France by the name of Arsène Lupin written by Maurice Leblanc. These books were very popular and people loved the kind thief who helped poor people by stealing valuable jewellery from the rich. I thought of him as a charitable man and would have liked to have been his assistant. My passionate goal in life is to help people in need. An Iraqi girl called Mona, wrote about becoming a nurse so that she could care for Iraqi soldiers in their war against the Jews. I was given the top marks in the class for my essay and the teacher told Mona, whose essay was in second place, that she hoped there would not still be fighting by the time she became a nurse; little did she know how events would transpire. I do not know whether Mona ever started her nursing training, and I doubted whether rich girls in Baghdad would ever become nurses. That same girl, who was supposed to be one of my friends, spread the word that it was not safe to have me in their houses as I could easily want to copy my hero! This was hurtful, and I suppose I could have been called, "The Thief of Baghdad;" there was a famous character in a movie with that title. That thought made me happy and I decided to convey these ideas to Mona. I thought we would have a laugh together, but instead she looked at me sourly and said that she could have me locked up as her uncle was the Chief of Police. I was worried at that news and imagined seeing the headlines in the newspapers, "Schoolgirl claims to be reincarnation of The Thief of Baghdad.

For the safety of the public she should be behind bars!" Even though I was only eleven years old I contemplated running away but where to? It was summer time and very hot. When I told my parents the story they did not find it amusing or laugh to make me feel better, but they did reassure me that I would not be going to jail. That was a relief, even though I was not fully convinced until a month had passed by.

From this time on, my father's words came true. We all had a sense of insecurity and I think this stemmed from the behaviour of our parents. We had heard that Iraq was sending soldiers to help the Arabs who were fighting the Jews in Palestine. The radio would be blaring with songs and poems containing hateful messages which stated that they would destroy the State of Israel, drive the people into the sea and there would be no Moses to part the waters. There was even a film made to inflame the entire Arab nation. Every day life was becoming more unpleasant for us but we continued to try and carry on as usual. It was very strange and also sad as to what was happening and, most of all, the confusion as what to do next. We did not know what was in store for us. It was as if a fire was breaking out and we were powerless to do anything about it. If we were to depart we realised that once we had left our home we would never see it again.

It was in 1948 that the State of Israel was founded.[5] Stories of imprisonment, fines, violence and even murder were commonplace and fear spread throughout the Jewish population. Things were not going to get better now and a flight to the new State of Israel became an unavoidable necessity. My parents, uncles and aunts decided that the children should go first. The authorities were making it difficult for Jews to leave the country. Those who could afford to pay would be allowed out first. It was decided that in the first instance my cousins and I should be given lessons in Modern Hebrew in order to prepare us for our arrival in Israel. The Hebrew teacher came to my uncle's house and we started the lessons. My cousin Yeheskel was independently minded, to say the least, and for some reason he took a dislike to the teacher. After a few lessons he put a spoonful of pepper into his coffee and that was the end of our Hebrew lessons. Uncle Abraham, my mother's brother had four boys. He was a successful businessman but became frightened that he would be targeted by Government forces, attacked because he was Jewish or to have his home and possessions confiscated as was frequently happening. He had a large house, and he also had connections abroad to do with his business and that was a dangerous situation. He saw that he was in peril without having done anything wrong. He took the right option. I often wondered if he was amused by the fact that he would never be pestered by my father about the money he was supposed to owe him. He and his whole family escaped to Tehran and I met them again in later years when the four boys emigrated to Israel. It was at this time that a Jew in Basra was hung in front of his house. He was accused of being a Zionist, without foundation. The Government claimed that they had their own information and that this would be an example for the Zionists. The main aim was to confiscate everything he owned and especially his properties. The morale of the Jews in Iraq reached a low on that day. Not all the Iraqi Jews went to Israel, some fled to England and the U.S.A. That was the end of our happy period on the rivers of Babylon. The curtains came down on what had been a pleasant play with a tragic ending.

At this time as Israel was about to be established, there were many angry demonstrations in Baghdad demanding that the idea of a State of Israel should not be permitted. People gathered in the streets shouting "Death to the Jews". These demonstrations could become violent and could erupt without any warning. We tried to keep out of the way but unfortunately, on one occasion, I was caught up in such an outburst and was very frightened. My best option was to join in before I was discovered and trampled on and there would be one Jew less! I started to chant we will win, or something of the sort. It must have sounded authentic because I was suddenly lifted up in the air on shoulders as the leader. I had no idea what my next move should be when suddenly there was an announcement on a loudspeaker for the crowd to disperse and move on to the main square. I was dropped to the ground without warning and not too gently. As the crowd melted away I managed to walk slowly without being observed. I put my head down and took the first turning I could find and I managed to get home as quickly as my legs could carry me. There was apparently going to be a search party looking for me organised by one of my cousins as it was dangerous to be out on days like these when the crowds would become frenzied and there was no telling what they would do in the name of a Jihad. The cousins were pondering which direction they should go to look for me. They became excited about how they were going to save their helpless cousin before it was too late. My sudden appearance was a shock for them. I wasn't sure whether they were happy to see me or disappointed that I had stopped their adventure. I felt like superman or superwoman. I told my family the story, feeling very proud of myself for surviving. My heroic story made me very popular for a long while!

At school I had been studying hard for the Primary Baccalaureate which is taken around the age of eleven. All the schools took the examination in a large hall and not in our own schools. Amongst the subjects I took were English, Arabic, mathematics, history and geography. My mathematics was always weak so I was surprised when the results showed that I received the top marks in Baghdad for the whole exam, and this was printed in the newspaper. That was one of the very few occasions when I saw my father show any emotion. He even went to collect my results in order to make sure it was all in order. I was not sure whether he was proud and pleased for me, or because he had received value for the money he spent on my private education. I did receive a reward of some extra pocket money but no kiss or hug. It felt like it was a business transaction.

On the announcement of the birth of Israel, Huda, my classmate and long term friend, requested not to sit next to me as I was Jewish. Going home from school that day her chauffeur scared me by aiming their car at me so that I jumped away from the road to the safety of the pavement. This was very upsetting to me, so I sat next to a Jewish girl in the class.

My spare time was spent with my three girl cousins next door and at the cinema where I saw Arabic and American movies. On a summer's evening when it was a little cooler, I liked open air cinemas and the ice creams that were sold there. I read numerous magazines and books. The eldest of my girl cousins was Daisy. She was about five years older than me and very elegant. She was an admirer of the latest fashions and she was always very caring towards me. I spent so much time at her house that it was said that her father, Uncle Matook, had four daughters instead of three. I called Uncle Matook, Papa. He had a generous and loving nature. He was not well educated but he was very kind to me, however, my father did not have a high opinion of him. The next daughter was Doris and we were very close, in fact, we were inseparable and went everywhere together. There was no question of any of the girls going out with boys. This just did not happen in our community. There was a boy who stood outside his house who we passed on our way to school. We admired him but he ignored our presence as if we did not exist. Another special friend was my cousin Myrna. She was younger than me but we always enjoyed each other's company. She was the daughter of Uncle Sassoon, my father's brother. She had a younger brother, Yossi, known as Joe, who I would carry on my back for walks and a younger sister, Judy, who I pampered when she was a baby.

FIVE

Escape to Israel

It was in March 1950 that a law was passed to allow Jews to leave Iraq, but in order to do this they had to surrender their Iraqi nationality and pay a large sum of money to the State, so this meant that poorer people were unable to leave the country. Later, the law was relaxed and people emigrated to Israel in larger numbers. The time had now arrived for me and many children to leave Iraq. The date was agreed by my parents, uncles and aunts and carrying a small bag I went with my father to the synagogue where we were all to meet. After a long wait we were told there was a delay and we had to return home. While waiting at home I fell asleep and was wakened in the night by my cousin Daisy who said it was time to go, and we crept out of the house without waking my parents, so no goodbyes were spoken. At the synagogue a bus was waiting to take us to the airport. After much excitement we boarded the 'plane which was packed with the migrant Jews and we flew to Cyprus. The 'plane bumped a great deal and many people were sick. In Cyprus we left the 'plane and waited in the airport until an Israeli 'plane arrived which we all boarded and flew to Tel Aviv, Israel. This 'plane was just as rickety as the previous one, however, we arrived safely. During the flight Doris and I remembered the things that we used to do in Baghdad, all the friends that we did not have a chance to say our farewells to, and whether we would meet them again in Israel. I told Doris that she would not be able to boss me about like she did in Baghdad. Doris would play many tricks on me such as suggesting we played strenuous games on a day that we were going to a party. I would tell her that I was tired and did not feel like playing games before going out. She would just smile but when we arrived at the party and saw some delicious cakes being offered to us she would stop the lady from giving me any as she explained that I was tired and the cakes might not agree with me. The lady would look pityingly at me and offered my cake to my caring and cunning cousin. I was so shocked and upset that I could not utter a word. I could have gladly strangled Doris as she had managed to out-manoeuvre me once again. Doris would not reveal much about herself. It was always hard to know what she was thinking, although she always seemed to know what I thought about everything. I was an open book to her and it was not easy to keep any secrets from her. She was a mystery that was hard to solve. It would have been difficult for Sherlock Holmes to discover the way through the maze that was inside her devious machinations. In her graduation school book it was written that, "She comes and goes and nobody knows." As the years went by I learned to anticipate Doris's tricks, and our friendship continues to this day. I am glad to say that she has been very happy for a long time with a loving husband, and she is now a young great-grandmother.

PART TWO

ISRAEL

SIX

Reception

On arrival at Lod Airport – later named *Ben Gurion Airport* to honour the first Prime Minister of Israel – and after the immigration procedures, we were transferred to trucks for a two hour drive to a reception centre near Haifa called a Mabara. It was near the sea with lovely sandy beaches. The sea was so inviting as it was calm and blue and I am sure that the water would have been warm as it was still September but, unfortunately, we were in an enclosed compound and could not get to the beach. It was a very strange feeling to be closed in. It was for a reason; security was very important in these early days and it was not advisable for the new arrivals to wander around. There were guards at each gate and special passes were needed for people who had to get out for an important reason, and even then, they had a limited time out of the compound. There were no exceptions to the rules and the security guards observed rigid precautions. From an early stage everyone realised that it was necessary to be united and obey the laws so that the newly born country would survive. We were no longer living on foreign soil! Life had been hectic and things had been moving so fast that there had been no time to stop and think, with all the excitement of getting away and travelling on an aeroplane for the very first time. As the big gate to the compound closed behind us, it suddenly occurred to me that I had left all my beloved books and movie magazines behind. In my confused mind I thought to myself that I should ask my parents to give them all to someone who would appreciate them. Of course, I forgot that there would be no communications as there was no such thing as mail between the two countries as Iraq would not permit any communications from Israel. I also remembered that I did not say goodbye to my lovely cat Minnie. Surely she would miss me when she didn't find me in bed in the morning or hear me calling her. I never thought about Minnie as having feelings of happiness or sadness but I suppose she must have had some. I had considered my departure as a big adventure and surely there would be peace at some time with the possibility of a return visit, but at the same time I realised that this was just a dream. Perhaps I should have smuggled Minnie with me and this would surely have made some headlines. Anyhow, I remembered that my parents would be looking after her. It was a strange feeling and suddenly my eyes misted with tears for the first time. There were no celebrations as we were all so tired and hungry. It was the eve of Yom Kippur (the Day of Atonement) on which we fast so this meant that hungry as we were, there was to be no food for the next twenty-four hours. At first there was chaos at the reception centre as many other people were arriving from different countries, speaking many languages and adding to the confusion. In addition there was not enough staff to cope with the large numbers. My cousins and I were given a hut to share; we had beds and showers and the conditions were better than the tents in which many had to stay. By the time we were allocated to our huts and our beds, I was so tired I even forgot about my hunger and I just fell into a deep sleep. I think I was too tired to dream that night, but if I did it would have been about food because I suddenly woke up with the movement of my jaw and I felt more hungry than ever.

The next evening we queued for food which we took back to our hut. It was not what we were used to but it was adequate. From then on we queued at breakfast, lunch and evening meal and became used to the basic provisions. There was a queue for everything in the compound. It was to establish order amongst the people so there would be no chaos. The word queue became a big joke among all the new arrivals. During conversations we would ask each other to say, "Please" if one wanted to air an opinion or speak. This always produced a laugh and kept the atmosphere light and cheerful whilst we waited to be given our destinations. We were not allowed out of the encampment area which was guarded day and night for security reasons, and we stayed there for some weeks until our future fate was decided. Whilst there my sense of adventure got the better of me and I kept thinking of ways to get out of the encampment area. The outside was so enticing that I could not wait to see the town of Haifa and Mount Carmel. There was so much to see and do.

When we left Baghdad we each had a suitcase and the equivalent of £30 each. Daisy kept the money, apart from a small amount which Doris and I had concealed. We would be able to enjoy ourselves if we could get out. I told Doris of my thoughts and she agreed, but we needed to keep this idea a secret, especially from Daisy, as she was our leader and would have definitely disapproved. We had to hatch a plan to get out. We studied the compound carefully for an outlet and found a small gate that could be opened from the outside and which was used by maintenance men. Delivery trucks came to the main gate; they unloaded their goods into small trucks to take to different parts of the camp. Usually there were a number of older children helping with the unloading in order to get a reward of some sweets. This proved to be the answer to our problem. We prepared ourselves and joined the group of volunteers helping with the unloading. We waited for things to get busy before we slipped away. It was a challenge and we took it. It was such an exciting feeling to see all the new sights around us in the town. We ate ice creams in the street and watched people shopping and families going to their homes together. It brought back memories because we were so far from our home. The excitement was tinged with sadness. We were bewildered as to what we were doing in these strange streets where we knew no one. We were far away from everything we knew and the experience was unreal. We heard the sound of music and voices singing a patriotic song about our land. I told myself that this was the answer because this was our home now and we should not question our fate. As we did not know our way around we did not wander too far. We did not want to abuse our freedom and we soon turned back It was with difficulty that we found the little gate and re-entered the encampment. We had an exhilarating sense of achievement for having accomplished our dream adventure. We went to find Daisy in case she was looking for us and when we met her she thought we smelled of ice cream! We looked rather uncomfortable but assured her that in no way would we have had ice cream without including her in the treat. We would not have enjoyed such pleasure without her sharing it with us. We put on a sad expression and she was very touched. Later we congratulated ourselves on a fine piece of acting, probably due to all the movies we had seen.

Babies were born in the camp during this time and the occasions were celebrated with singing and dancing. They were called "Sabras" meaning they were born in Israel. Sabra is a fruit which is prickly on the outside but soft on the inside. That is how the Israelis describe themselves. They might be rough and loud to deal with at times but they mellow quickly if handled gently. They are never completely relaxed because of the continuous tension in the country about remaining safe in the midst of so many dangers. We became acquainted with other refugees as time went by, and mixed with those we could talk to and who we liked. The problem was that very few of the arrivals spoke Hebrew and so conversation could be very hesitant as we all struggled to learn some words of what was to be our common tongue. At times it was amusing to see how everyone tried to make other people understand their own language. Some used signs and pointed at different things to try and explain themselves. There were at least ten different languages spoken on the Kibbutz. The next move was to another reception camp in a town called Hadera. The allocations were given after taking into consideration all the various factors in our past experiences, ages and backgrounds. My cousin Daisy, who was interested in social care, was sent to Jerusalem to study social services. My cousin Yeheskel went to the Army but not willingly. He had changed from the moment that we arrived. His patriotic spirit vanished. It was not what he expected. Whilst everybody around him tried to make the most of things in order to have a new start, he could not conform. He had been spoiled at home where he was the only boy among four children and he suddenly found himself in a situation where he was no longer someone special. He had been the focus of attention at home and took advantage of this adoration by his weak parents resulting in a false sense of his own importance. It was interesting to watch him now as he had no way out of his present position.

Doris and I were assigned to Kibbutzim. It was intended that I should go to a Kibbutz where there would only be two hours of work a day and school lessons for the rest of the time. Doris, who was a little older than me, was to go to a Kibbutz where she would work slightly longer hours. I protested that I did not want to be separated from Doris and that I was prepared to work longer hours. My protests were successful and Doris and I were sent to Kibbutz Ein Harod in Northern Israel, near the town of Afula. This kibbutz was founded in 1921. Shortly after Doris and I left, it was split into two kibbutzim. It was in a beautiful location overlooking Mount Herman and it was a luxury kibbutz compared with many.

SEVEN

Kibbutz

On arrival at the kibbutz we were given a warm welcome and Doris and I, and two sisters called Shoshana and Dahlia were sent to a four-bedded hut. Shoshana and Dahlia were also from Iraq; they came from a poor family and had received little education. There were four beds in one large room with desks and cupboards, and the bathrooms had showers and sinks. Our meals were in a dining hall where the adults served us and washed up. There were three meals a day: for breakfast we had salads, fish, cottage cheese, freshly baked bread and orange juice. On Saturday we had an egg. Eggs were in short supply and soldiers had priority. For lunches and evening meals we usually had hot food. Meat was limited but there was an ample supply of vegetables and fruit. Although there was no rationing in the Kibbutz, we were dependent on what was available. Passover was a special occasion when everyone sat at long tables in the open air during the service. Life was well organised on our Kibbutz with rules for almost everything one did and if you abode by them life could be very pleasant. However, for some there would always be thoughts of other longings and what was going on in the outside world. We worked in the fields either in the mornings or in the afternoons. I would work alongside a boy called Elli and he would tell me stories as we worked. He and his sister came from Iraq; she had been in love with a Moslem boy. This was unusual for a Jewish girl and likewise for the boy resulting in forbidden love. The brother, although he was young at the time, reluctantly became the go-between. In this way he could keep watch on his sister whom he loved very much. He realised how determined she was to keep in touch with this boy who had good looks as well as having a nice personality. He came from a very respectable family. The problem which they had to overcome was their religion and their brief meetings had to be accomplished like a military operation. When she came to Israel he left Iraq and moved to Jordan to be nearer to her. He had no wish to live without her but they could not correspond because of the war between Jordan and Israel, so she would write imaginary letters to him which she never posted. I do not know what happened to her but I do not think they ever got together again, so their love was doomed and their story was a sad one. I liked the stories that Elli told me while we were working but this particular one made me rather tearful. Life has its own way of planning for us, so who knows they might meet one day.

The work on the Kibbutz involved digging up carrots and potatoes, or picking oranges and grapefruits from the trees. Every day our representative would find out which duties we each had to do and received the protests of those who were not happy with their allotted work. The other half of the day was spent in the school where we studied Hebrew, history, geography and biblical studies. All the lessons were given in Hebrew and of necessity we had to learn the language quickly so that the thirty different languages being spoken could be replaced by one common one. Somehow Doris and I picked up the language easily. There was a swimming pool which I used occasionally, and we had a cinema which showed a film once a month. Doris and I, with our knowledge of English, could explain the films to the others who would gather around us to hear our translations into Hebrew. In the grounds there was a dental surgery and a medical clinic. There was always a lot to do and we girls always had a lot of fun. We would visit other huts and play games. In the event of there being a shortage of activities to enjoy, Doris and I would provide imaginary scandalous stories to excite the other girls. In the evenings there was usually some entertainment in the dining hall. We performed plays and sometimes soldiers would arrive to give concerts, and we enjoyed many other activities. The security for the Kibbutz was provided by soldiers and we knew them all. Throughout my time on the Kibbutz and later in Haifa, we were all aware of the possible dangers from terrorists, since the surrounding Arab countries had made it quite clear that they wished to eliminate the State of Israel. Unlike the Jews who were establishing a home in Israel, the Arabs in the surrounding lands were refused integration by their hosts. As a consequence, hostile acts were commonplace and we needed to be vigilant in our everyday activities. The Palestinian problem was frequently on my mind. It seemed wrong that they should be living in refugee camps with the new generations born to hate the Jews. They lived under the illusion that the surrounding Arab countries would come to their rescue. Hate can make people so angry and violent. I used to think miracles could happen so that there could be peace. Hopefully, one day there will be a solution to the problem that has been going on for so long.

Doris and I were well known in the Kibbutz. We had received a better education than most of the girls of our age and we could engage easily with the children, adults and teachers. Dahlia was the elder and more attractive of the two sisters who shared our hut. They both had a sweet nature and Doris and I enjoyed teasing them, especially the younger one.

We told Shoshana one day that one of the boys was crazy about her. She went up to him and told him that she was crazy about him too. He said, "What are you talking about, I don't even like girls." Shoshana, being rebuffed, was next seen outside the dining hall with a table knife in her hand. One of the teachers named Harmon asked Shoshana what was the matter as she seemed distressed, and she told him she was going to kill those two (me and my cousin Doris). Harmon told her to calm down and when he saw us he advised us to be careful as he didn't want any murders on the kibbutz. We told him not to worry as we would sort things out. We told Shoshana not to be upset as the boy was not worthy of her, and we said, in fact, it was his brother who liked her but not to approach him as he would be influenced by the brother who had rejected her. We told her that there were dozens of boys in the Kibbutz who would love to be friendly with her; this appeased her and she replaced the knife on the dining room table and hugged us. She was a lovely person whom we loved but although we were her heroes, we just could not resist teasing her.

Some of the girls missed their parents and were homesick. There was one girl who cried daily. Sometimes the tears would roll down her cheeks and one day I offered her a towel. In my mind this was a joke but she thanked me sincerely for the gesture. My cousin Daisy came from Jerusalem to visit Doris and me a few times. Her brother Yeheskel came once in Army uniform, together with a soldier friend. They did not come to visit for their love of us but rather for the good and fresh food they could have on the Kibbutz, as well as ogling the girls. As soldiers, they were allowed to stay a few days and Doris and I hardly saw them. Yeheskel was not happy in the Army and in some ways I felt sorry for him. Daisy told us that she had heard that two more cousins of ours had arrived at another Kibbutz,

Doris and I visited them travelling on a milk cart and stayed with them at their kibbutz for a few days. After that, we were informed that our stay had ended and we had to go back to our Kibbutz. We said our farewells to the cousins and then faced the problem of our return. Apparently, the milk cart was not going back for some time. We should have found out how we were going to return when we asked permission to visit. Our Kibbutz was eventually contacted and reluctantly we were given some bus money and some food. It was a long walk to the bus stop and a long wait. It was hot, our water was running out and the whole experience was not pleasant. I felt sorry for myself and needless to say we were not greeted with a hero's welcome when we returned.

My thoughts during the days at the reception centre were so occupied with all the new events that I had little time to think about home. Once in the kibbutz I was happy and I was never homesick. My father had never showed me affection and my mother was remote because of her depression, so I did not miss them. However, I sometimes thought about our house and the good times I had enjoyed in Baghdad, but I would never show that I cared about missing my old life because I had no time for weakness and I was always determined to survive.

EIGHT

Haifa

In Haifa, a prominent sea port in the north of Israel, I had cousins who owned a large Arab house which they had purchased in the days of Palestine. It was not uncommon in those days long before the State of Israel was founded, for residents to sell property to the Jews and that is how my mother's rich cousins came to own property in Haifa. The husband and wife were themselves cousins and both were related to my mother. He was part of a rich family who had invested in property on Mount Carmel whilst they lived in Baghdad. Mount Carmel rose above Haifa and their house was situated toward the upper region of Mount Carmel. Nearby there were fine views over the town, the Mediterranean, and even Lebanon to the north. Our families were in touch with them as we had all known each other in Baghdad before we had emigrated. When they heard we were on a kibbutz they were keen for Doris and me to come and live with them. They claimed that two young girls should be with family and not alone on a kibbutz, and it would be nice for the family to have Doris and me to join them as they had recently arrived in the country and did not speak Hebrew. They had three children and thought that we would be able to help with their education. This sounded exciting for us. We were going to miss all our friends and we knew that there was going to be much more responsibility for us living outside the security of the kibbutz where we did not have to worry about possessions and were protected in every way. We took up the invitation and before we went to Haifa we were moved to another kibbutz for a short while; we then travelled to Haifa by bus and found their house. It was in large grounds and next to it there was a cottage, a filling station and two smaller buildings which were single room apartments, and all of them belonging to my cousins. We were given a room in the house which we shared with one of their girls. The names of their girls were Simcha and Haluna and the boy was called Yeheskel. I spent a few sleepless nights wondering whether we made the right decision. Our relatives were very religious. They were kind and fond of us but I shall always remember with fond memories my time in the Kibbutz. I wanted to be in the outside world and try to plan my future and this was a challenge for me.

Doris and I soon settled in the house. We ate with the family and found jobs in a hotel as chambermaids for the summer. The hotel was called "Carmelia" and was situated between the house and the port. We enjoyed the work and found plenty to giggle about. It is surprising how much you could learn about people from the guests who were staying in the hotel. You could tell the married couples who seemed to be relaxed, although some were displaying signs of boredom with each other's company by choosing different destinations for sightseeing. Then there were the holiday affair couples who were rather edgy, perhaps with feelings of guilt which made one uncomfortable to look at them. It seemed as if we shared a secret. They were very generous with their tips which were welcomed by us. It was hardly up to us to make judgements, especially as we did not really know about their circumstances. At home we helped the girls with their homework. They found everything very difficult and it was hard work teaching them. They had a little brother who was a "terror" and threatened us with dire fates, such as removing our eyes, but we managed to ignore him most of the time. (*I met him years later when he was grown up and I heard that he was working in a jeweller's shop in London. I walked in pretending to sell a piece of jewellery; he did not recognise me and offered me a price. I informed him that he was a cheat and that the earrings were worth much more and that I needed the money badly. He frowned and seemed puzzled. I had to laugh and he suddenly recognised me. It was an unusual meeting.*)

After a while, we left the hotel and began to work as waitresses in restaurants in the port in the evenings, and also attended typing school in the daytime. The clientele of the restaurants were mainly sailors and the restaurants tended to be Greek. The sailors were of many nationalities and concentrated more on drink than on food. Doris and I liked the work because the atmosphere was lively and friendly. I always believed in doing my very best at whatever I tackled and I liked to be cheerful with everyone, not just because that attitude improved the tips, but also because I saw no point being miserable in a job, especially as I knew it was only a temporary position. Apart from serving the food which was limited because of rationing, we would bring beer and Arak from the bar to the rowdy sailors. On one occasion a group of about ten sailors walked out without paying their bill. The boss when he heard this put his head in his hands and moaned. I ran out of the restaurant and caught up with the sailors on the quayside. They apologised and started turning out their pockets. I held my apron out and they piled many notes and coins into it. When I returned to the restaurant the boss started to count the money and found they had paid much more than the total bill. The boss said we could share the extra between us and gave me a peck on the forehead. His wife, who was very jealous because he had a reputation for flirting with ladies, came over to investigate but soon realised that there was nothing to the whole matter. His wife usually stood opposite the restaurant at closing time to watch what was going on and her husband's behaviour. I must say that the boss never flirted with any of the waitresses; it was always strictly business with us.

Doris and I now heard that our mothers' brother and sister, Uncle Nissim and Aunt Lulu, had arrived in Israel and were in a reception camp. We were very surprised to hear that this elderly uncle and aunt who had never travelled in their lives before had been transferred to such a different environment. They must have been undergoing a horrendous experience. We were very fond of them in Baghdad and, apparently, they were sent ahead by Doris's parents until they could be claimed. In the meantime, their situation was worrying because they might be sent to a home for misplaced persons in a remote part of the country. We became distressed at the thought of this happening to them. One day, Doris and I travelled by bus to visit them and they were very pleased to see us. They were elderly, lonely and frightened and had been given a tent erected on sand. They pleaded with us to get them away from the camp and seeing them in that state upset us. We could envisage them being taken to a home. Israel was having a hard time coping with the influx of people pouring in from all over. Doris and I decided to try our best to help them and we reassured them. We visited them several times taking them food which we bought with our small earnings. Back in the house in Haifa, we asked our relatives if they would consider helping but the problem was that there were already several elderly relatives living in the small cottages and outhouses in the grounds, and they felt that the area was becoming an old people's home. We told our cousins that we would like to move out of the house into one of the small buildings in the grounds and we promised to clean it up and make it habitable. Doris found the key and we obtained permission from the brother of the owners, who managed the estate for them, to bring Nissim and Lulu there. The next task was to furnish the place. It was hard to know where to start and a big challenge to prove that we were capable of going through with what we had started. We targeted certain people that we knew could help, some were complete strangers, some were shop owners, and any others who could give donations. We also offered to do any jobs that were available. The story of our need to rescue our uncle and aunt was a great asset as well as the sorrowful look on our faces when we described their condition. The story was leaked to the local paper and when we had reached our goal we were delighted with the results. Doris wrote a short poem of thanks for all the kindness we had received which was also published in the local paper. When we next visited them they wanted to know how many days it would be before we came to collect them. Uncle Nissim, who was illiterate, had already started to count the days by making marks in the sand outside their tent. They had told the other old people in the camp that these two young nieces were going to take them away and there had been much laughter at the unlikelihood of such an event. After saving some more money from our work at the restaurants, we managed to hire a horse and cart and arrived at the camp. Whilst our uncle and aunt boarded the cart with their suitcases, together with Doris and I, there was great excitement in the camp and many old people were clapping and shouting their farewells, whilst my uncle and aunt waved to the crowd as if they were royalty. It was a very emotional scene; to see the joy on the faces of those two dear old people would have made a very pretty picture, alas we did not have a camera. The horse and cart took us back to Haifa and from there we boarded a bus to Mount Carmel. This memorable event in my life was worth all the effort, both physical and emotional, that we had devoted to it.

Uncle Nissim moved into the main house to share a room with two other elderly male relatives. Aunt Lulu moved in with Doris and me. Aunt Lulu was a good cook and she made us some tasty dishes. Uncle Nissim would pass by and complain that she used too much salt. The two of them were always arguing. Uncle Nissim was a bachelor and a strictly Orthodox Jew. He prayed several times a day but this did not prevent him from any shrewd deals he could achieve. Life seemed to be busy for Uncle Nissim since his arrival. I never discovered what kept him busy, but it was a pleasure to see him happy. In the room with him was a cousin called Nissim Nissim. Uncle's name was Nissim Saul. One day the social services lady arrived to give a pension book to Nissim Nissim. My uncle claimed the book and started to receive the pension. When Nissim Nissim discovered what had happened he was furious. He had been waiting for weeks for his pension and now it had been taken by a new arrival. My uncle protested that it was a mistake and he had thought it was intended for him, but it took some time for everything to be sorted out and calm to be restored.

At this time, Doris's parents arrived in Israel and found an apartment in Givatayim, near Tel Aviv. We went to join them but the apartment became so crowded that I could not stay any longer and I returned to Haifa. I had begun to think about my future. At school in Baghdad I had been interested in journalism and hoped to go to the American University in Beirut, Lebanon, but this was not to be, and in Israel my thoughts moved towards nursing. My cousin Sabiha, whose house we lived in, was possessive and Doris and I found that she was always trying to direct our lives. She wanted to keep us close at hand and I began to dream of getting away from it all, especially as my parents were showing no signs of leaving Baghdad. I enquired about training to be a nurse in Israel but was told that I needed many preliminary qualifications and there was also a waiting list of five hundred wishing to train as nurses. My father had always talked about educational standards in England being very high, so I began to explore that possibility. I knew that it was like reaching for the stars. I had no idea how and where to start. I became obsessed with the idea and decided to give it all my attention. After all, how can a dream come true if you don't dream? In the first place, I decided to improve my English. I found a Catholic school which offered free English lessons in return for some Hebrew lessons for the young ones, and there I met Frère Benoit who was very kind, and with him I continued my English studies. Although the lessons were free, I gave the school a donation from my earnings. Frère Benoit became a good friend to me; someone I could talk to and confide in. This was not easy for me to do with anyone else, and consequently our conversations were a great relief for me. He was in his late thirties and dedicated to his work with young people. Frère Benoit followed my progress in working to achieve my dream and he was very pleased when I was successful, but this meant that we now had to say farewell. It was not an easy thing to do as I had come to rely on his advice and emotional support. This meant a lot to me as I had never had anyone I could talk to in that manner. It was so comforting to have someone's genuine attention. We agreed to correspond so that I could tell him of my new life in England. I set about applying for a passport without telling my cousin Sabiha. In fact, the only one who knew my intentions was Doris who was spending her time between Givatayim and Haifa. My passport application duly arrived but when I approached Sabiha and pleaded with her to countersign it as it was my dream to travel to England and train as a nurse, she replied that I did not need to travel abroad and that if I did so I would end up being converted to Christianity, whereupon she destroyed the papers and left me feeling angry and aggrieved. Sabiha envisaged that there were no Jews anywhere except in Israel and Baghdad. I had to find a way to get a passport and go through the bureaucracy again. In those days it was difficult to obtain a passport and so it became a big challenge for me. It was going to be a long and hard struggle so I had to think fast as, apart from my desire to enter a nursing school in England, I was approaching the military service age. It had to be a fool-proof plan using both my intelligence and determination. I needed to be cool and calculating in order to avoid any mistakes. I knew Uncle Nissim wanted to belong to the National Insurance Scheme as soon as he could. I thought that this was my one and only chance for a close relative to sign my application. He did not know when I took him to the Passport Office that it was not the National Insurance Office. I was very nervous as this was a risky game I was playing. I thought that I could be arrested for the deception and that there were so many obstacles in front of me. Arriving at the Passport Office, I found the people at the reception desk were not sympathetic and very matter-of-fact, perhaps because they did not want young persons of military age to leave the country. I completed a new application whilst wondering if the officials could hear my heart thumping. I confirmed that my uncle was happy for me to travel for a while. Although he could read Biblical Hebrew he did not understand Modern Hebrew and I told him that I was registering him for national insurance to cover his medical needs. I was asked many questions and then my height was measured standing in front of a wooden post marked in centimetres. Uncle Nissim asked why I was being measured if it was his National Insurance. I told him that they were measuring me because I was his sponsor. He then signed my forms believing it was his own National Insurance application. This episode in my life was unforgettable as something could have gone wrong at any minute in that office, especially when uncle had to sign his approval. Uncle Nissim was illiterate and could not sign his name, but he kept his dignity by informing the official that he always signed with his thumb when required. To my great relief, he nodded and passed over the ink. There, at last, was his signature and the dated line. I never thought I would have such a pleasant encounter with a thumb! I could not allow myself a sigh of relief. We left the Passport Office and it was certainly a very tense moment for me as I was sure I would be called back, but here I was outside the building and I had made it! Uncle Nissim was very pleased and gave me money for an ice cream. This time I was not going to let Sabiha near my passport. I felt some guilt about deceiving Uncle Nissim, but I knew he would automatically get his national insurance pension in due course.

One day, whilst walking on Mount Carmel, I met two English ladies who asked me for directions. I walked part of the way with them and we arranged to meet again for coffee. At that time I was working in restaurants in the evenings and studying English during the day. When we met again, I told them about my dream to travel to England and train as a nurse, and I also told them how unhappy I had been living with Sabiha and how she had tried to stop me leaving. They were very interested in helping me and introduced me to a children's home where I could work and also be given accommodation.

They also said that they would write to a friend in England who was on the Board of Governors of the Kent and Canterbury Hospitals. I took up the job at the children's home where children of single mothers, or of parents who were working, spent the day and sometimes boarded. I enjoyed this work and at the same time I was continuing with my English lessons. The children at the home were very sweet. I loved them and they loved me in return. For the first time in a long while I felt relaxed and happy amongst these lovely children, and it was all great fun. One of the children used to call another child fat, but when I stopped him saying that, he would walk around with his cheeks blown up every time he passed that boy. It showed a good sense of humour since he was only six years old. I then went to live with a Canadian lady who had been introduced to me by the English ladies.

Whilst I was waiting for the result of my passport application, my Uncle Sassoon arrived with his family from Baghdad. He brought some money for me from my father who said that it was only to be used for emergencies. Knowing my father, that meant not to use it. Although I was very close to Uncle Sassoon, I did not tell him of my plans in case he tried to dissuade me from leaving Israel. After a short while in Haifa, he moved to Tel Aviv. It was not easy to lead a double life. I did not like to be secretive; I found it very hard, especially with people close to me. I would have loved to have declared my ambitions and determination about what I wanted to do, but I had no option. I could not take the risk of exposing my plans to my uncle. However, I did not feel guilty as I was following a dream to better myself and make my parents and the people that mattered proud of me, especially as my parents were still in Baghdad and I could not tell them of my plans. Somehow I knew they would have approved, so I was the one who was responsible for my actions and I had to make sure that I did not disclose my plans when I spoke to people. This could have easily happened in my excitement about the forthcoming departure. At times I was frustrated because I was so anxious to get away as fast as possible and yet I had to wait for my plans to come to fruition.

One day, a letter from the Governor of Kent and Canterbury Hospitals in England arrived enquiring about my desire to train as a nurse. I corresponded with him and was finally asked to write to the Matron of Margate and Ramsgate Hospitals. She asked me to write an essay on "Why I wanted to be a nurse". I accordingly sent her this essay and she replied saying that she was impressed and she would hold a place for me to start my preliminary training at her hospitals upon my arrival. I finally collected my passport and it now remained only to try and book my passage to England. Holding that passport in my hand was a euphoric moment for me. It was the most precious item I had ever owned. To keep it safe was my biggest concern and I even had some nightmares about losing it. I was still staying at the home of the Canadian lady. She was helping me to get away and as a gift she gave me a suitcase and I put the passport under the lining of the case and locked it with the key which I put on a chain around my neck, hidden under my shirt. These arrangements did not come naturally to me and the details were leaving me mentally exhausted. I was thinking about the project and my next move twenty-four hours a day. I wondered if that was how prisoners of war felt when they were trying to escape. I wanted to see all my family before I left Israel and so I went to Tel Aviv. I did not tell anyone, except Doris, that I was leaving as I did not want anything to interfere with my plans. I felt sad in a way as I had no idea if and when I would see them all again. My consolation was that I now had a few supporters outside of the family and I had to rely on them as well as my own endeavours. Once when I was with my cousin Daisy I passed a young man who worked in the Passport Office. He said, "Hello, haven't you gone yet?" I had a shock and ignored him and walked on. The poor man looked so hurt and Daisy wanted to know what it was all about. I put on the most innocent expression I could manage whilst denying that I knew him or knew what he meant. Obviously, he mistook me for someone else after all I didn't possess an unusual face. I managed to make Daisy laugh.

NINE

Journey to England

I returned to Haifa and began to look for the cheapest way to get to England. I had never travelled abroad on my own before, but I was determined to fulfil my ambition. Because of the offer I had received to train as a nurse, there was no problem with the British Authorities who gave me a visa to stay in England.

I made enquiries about various methods of transport and decided to get a ship from Haifa to Italy and then travel by train to London. The fare for the sea passage used most of the money I had saved, but after calculating how much I needed I thought I would have enough to pay for the train, although I would be left with very little. My new good friends in Haifa were generous to me with little gifts of money on my departure. I had to be very careful as to how to spend it. Unfortunately, I lost my purse in the Post Office and it broke my heart; I shed some tears which was most unlike me. I was so tired from trying to do everything myself, and losing my purse was the last straw. I thought to myself that perhaps I was being punished for what I was doing. However, I was certainly not doing anything wrong or harming anyone, but then I began to look at the funny side of the whole matter and I was relieved at the thought that somebody up on high was having a joke with me. This was not a time for morbid thoughts. People felt sorry for me and started to look for my purse. A kind lady saw a little boy playing with a purse and it turned out to be mine. I was so relieved that I celebrated by going to the cinema.

The passenger ship was very small compared with today's cruise liners. One day I would travel on a luxury cruise liner, but to me it did not hold the excitement of this humble little ship and all the dangers associated with my journey. As I climbed the gangway I felt unreal and that perhaps I should not have been there. The ship was getting ready to sail and people were standing on deck to wave goodbye to family and friends. I must have been the only one who was not waving. It was a relief when we finally set sail; I had made it, or so I thought! The ship plied Mediterranean ports and I was given a bunk in a four-berth cabin with a lady and her two daughters. They were heading for Venezuela where her husband had travelled ahead to start work. The mother was a pleasant lady and the eldest daughter, who was about sixteen, had a fine voice and entertained the passengers with songs in the evenings. The youngest daughter was about fourteen and was sea sick much of the time and unhappy. I think she did not want to leave Israel. Although it was the Mediterranean, the seas were fairly rough but luckily I was not upset by this and I think that was because I was so pleased to be on my way at last.

Our first port of call was Cyprus. It was near Christmas and we were joined by a group of British soldiers going on leave for the holidays. It was the 1950s and military service was still compulsory for young men: one of them, by the name of Derek Fletcher, talked to me and wanted to know what I was doing on an Italian ship. As I began to tell my story he asked for details and at first he thought I was joking and then he became intrigued and amazed at my exploits and my persistence in carrying out my desires. He told me that my arrangements for all of this were like a military operation. My story was not fictional and he was concerned for my safety. We sat talking late into the night and he told me about his service experiences and how he looked forward to his leave and seeing his parents again. After that, we talked together every day and it was very pleasant to be with a cheerful and gentlemanly person. I let myself believe that England would be full of Derek Fletchers. We arrived in Piraeus, the port for Athens in Greece and remained there for the day. Derek accompanied me on a tour of the Acropolis and the Temple of the Parthenon, and we then returned to the ship. It was a pleasure to be in his company and to relax and be myself. I thought I must write and tell Frère Benoit all about Derek when I get to my destination.

We next called at Naples in Italy, and finally reached Genoa. The passengers disembarked but when I reached the immigration authorities and told them I was going to catch a train to England I was informed that I could not travel through Italy as I did not have an Italian visa. I was told to return to the ship and be taken back to Haifa. Before leaving Israel I had not considered such a requirement. It was like a nightmare, surely this was not me they were talking to; it felt like I was watching someone else's misfortune. I was told that I would have to stay on the ship until it returned to Haifa. While all this was going on, Derek was standing nearby. I knew this was my only chance of getting away and I was in despair, but although the rest of his Company proceeded to head for home, Derek stayed behind to try and help me. He could see how distressed I was because he knew that once I returned I would never get another chance to leave. I was overwhelmed by Derek's caring and protective way towards me. There are no words to describe how I felt except to say that I was humble at such generous humanity. The words, "Thank you," seemed inadequate for such a kind person. What he did was amazing for someone I had only known for a few days.

Derek took me ashore again and consulted with the Italian authorities. He explained that I was too upset to comprehend what was going on and that it was essential that I should be allowed to continue my journey in order to start my studies on time. There must be a solution to the problem. There was a long debate and they then allowed me to have my passport stamped and make enquiries. They were sympathetic, but the only solution was for me to fly to England and not travel overland. The only flights would be from Milan and the authorities said that there would have to be a security officer on the train to Milan in order to ensure that I did not alight at any point. The earliest train would be the next day. I returned to the ship where I was allowed to stay overnight. It was not an ideal situation for me to be alone on the ship with the crew, so Derek said he would stay and he sat outside my cabin all night. He sang the French song "Alouette" and other songs, and I was very grateful for such a kind gesture. I was very emotional about the day's events and could not imagine what I would have done without Derek. I was so lucky, or was it fate, that he was to be on my ship. Not all angels have wings; I read that somewhere and with that thought I fell asleep.

The next day we went to the station, liaised with the security officer and I boarded the train. I think the security officer was expecting us to linger with our "goodbyes" and have a kiss or a hug in a romantic way like it happens when two young people say goodbye at stations. But to the disappointment of the security guard, none of these things happened. I was too emotional and shy to say or do anything apart from smiling my thanks. Some tears were gathering in my eyes but I held them back. Derek had to catch his own train back to London for his leave, before returning to his next duty in Malta. Derek predicted in his subsequent correspondence that I would make a very good nurse and would marry a nice doctor who would take good care of me. This prediction was to come true. Although I thanked Derek for his help and did, in fact, correspond with him for a while, I always felt that I should have been able to tell him how much I owed him, for without his help I would not be here today. I would still like to thank him face to face if I could contact him again; it is one of my dearest wishes. I tell my grandchildren how lucky I am to be here and having such lovely grandchildren, all six of them, and what a large part Derek played in making this possible.

The train journey to Milan was a short one of only a couple of hours. I went to the airport and enquired about a flight to London. I was told I had to change flights in Switzerland and the cost was more money than I had. This was another obstacle to overcome. The only person I could think of to possibly help me was the gentleman on the Board of Governors who had put me in touch with Margate Hospitals. With the help of an airline official I managed to call him and told him my predicament. I told him that my father would reimburse him, which he did later, and he arranged my ticket to London. Whilst waiting at the airport in Milan, I sat next to an elderly English lady who asked me where I was going. I told her that I was going to start training as a nurse at hospitals in Kent. She told me that she had trained as a nurse at St. Thomas's Hospital in London many years previously. Her name was Agnes Parkin-Moore, later to be known as Aunt Aggie. She told me about the connection between St. Thomas's Hospital and Florence Nightingale, who was a pioneering nurse during the Crimean War. She cared for wounded soldiers and was known as "The Lady of the Lamp". We sat next to each other on the 'plane and I asked her how I could get to London from the airport and then catch a train to Margate. Agnes told me that I might have a problem because it was Christmas and there would probably be no trains by the time I got to London. I said that I would sleep in the station until there was a train, but she said that a young lady could not do that and she invited me to her home to stay until the morning. After a brief landing in Switzerland we continued to London. As it was Christmas and there was a restricted train timetable, I had to stay more than one night. Aunt Aggie was an attractive lady, tall, slim and smartly dressed. I gathered that she came from an aristocratic family who were originally from Scotland. I was very impressed by the members of her family who I met in those few days.

PART THREE

ENGLAND

TEN

Arrival

Agnes lived in a flat in London, near Paddington station and made me feel at home. It was great to feel warm and safe, and it was heavenly to be able to have a hot bath. Next morning, I stood on the balcony and looked all around. I was in London at last, and I thought maybe I should pinch myself. Looking back now, I know how Oliver Twist must have felt, and I also think that I should have been singing, "If My Friends Could See Me Now", from the film "Sweet Charity". Before I left Italy, I had to leave my suitcase at the airport as collateral until they received the money for my flight. I took only the essentials. It certainly was an odd feeling to part with all my possessions that I had packed with loving care. I almost had the urge to say goodbye and hope to see you soon, and even give the suitcase a hug! Why not, it was my only possession but I refrained in case people would think I was a lunatic and have me locked up. Aunt Aggie suddenly realised that I didn't have much luggage with me. When I explained she shook her head and said, "Come on, we are going shopping." It was a fantastic experience to see the streets of London and the beautiful shops with their Christmas decorations. I called it a fairyland planet. Aunt Aggie bought me a beautiful dress and some other clothes. I was overwhelmed with such an act. Words failed me in trying to express my gratitude and I couldn't help a few silent tears. I was so proud to wear my dress in Aunt Aggie's company. I rated it the best dress I had ever owned.

After spending a very pleasant few days with Aunt Aggie, she arranged for us to travel together to the hospital in Margate where she would safely deliver me to the Matron and introduce herself. The train journey to Kent took us through beautiful scenery and we ate lunch in a luxurious dining car which was something I had never even imagined before. Agnes turned out to be my second guardian angel, taking me under her wing to enlighten me about England, English behaviour and ways. From the time of my arrival on these shores, I received nothing but kindness and generosity from her. Although I had been happy in Baghdad and on the kibbutz, and had made the best of my working experience in Haifa, I still wanted to do something more with my life. I felt that further study would help to give me some personal satisfaction as well as a career. I had been very lucky and if angels without wings existed, I had met two of them so far on my journey. I believe that somebody up there liked me. It was Christmas 1955; I was eighteen years of age and about to commence my nursing training in England.

ELEVEN

Margate/Ramsgate School of Nursing

Agnes and I arrived at Margate and went to the hospital where we were greeted by Matron. Agnes introduced us and enjoyed a conversation with Matron exchanging nursing reminiscences. Matron explained that I would enter a three-year course to become a State Registered Nurse and this would be preceded by a three-month course at a Preliminary Training School (P.T.S.) with examinations at the end of the course. She then gave us a brief tour of the hospital and Aunt Agnes left, promising that she would soon be in touch again. She gave me a tender, loving hug that had not come my way in the past. I could only utter the word "thanks". I seemed to have been using that word a lot over the last few days. It did not seem to be enough in order to express my feelings. There should have been a more expressive word. What had I done to deserve such kindness, and how did fate arrange that I met such extraordinary people?

The Home Sister in charge of accommodation showed me to my room. There were already three or four girls waiting to start P.T.S. in three days' time, and they, and the other seven girls who would start with me, would remain my friends for the next three years, and some of them to the present day. We all talked together excitedly as we discussed our futures and considered the documents about the P.T.S. and what we would be studying. There would be one day a week on the wards having practical experience; the rest of the time we would have lectures from the Sister Tutors and Hospital Doctors and these would take place in a separate building. We would be learning Anatomy, Physiology, Medicine and the Principles of Nursing. These were all new subjects for me. Two of the Sister Tutors asked me many questions and seemed to like me. One of the trainees in my group was Julie Wood, who in later years after becoming an air stewardess and then marrying, wrote a moving novel about an English village during the First World War.[6] She also wrote children's books. Other particular friends were Margaret Windle in my set, and three months behind me were Val and Barnie. We are still in contact after all these years. Everything was somewhat strange for me, especially getting used to the dialects and colloquial English employed by these young girls who were mainly from South East England, as my English came from an American School and American films. They, in turn, found my accent and explanations amusing, although I seemed to have better general knowledge than the other girls. We were given nursing uniforms and received a very small payment each month. This was not too important as our food and accommodation were provided for us. If we wished to stay out of the hospital until eleven p.m. we had to request a late pass.

As the P.T.S. got underway I found the studies quite difficult. It was a struggle to keep up with everyone and follow what was going on at a fast pace in English. I still had some way to go to improve my English but everyone was patient with me, especially the Sister Tutors. We were advised to concentrate on our three years of hard study and work, and not indulge in too many late nights. We were only allowed two off-duty passes a week anyway. Marriage was not permitted while in training, and socialising with patients was also not allowed in order to maintain the respectable image of a nurse. I began to get up at five a.m. to read my notes and the text books, but the night sister saw the light under my door and came in to see me. She wanted to know if I had been doing this every day and told me I should stop as I would be too tired to concentrate on my day time studies. As the weeks went by things became easier.

Sitting in the dining room one day, the two Sister Tutors who were so friendly towards me said that I was looking so much better since my arrival. My cheeks were filling out and becoming rosy instead of pale. Several of the girls heard them admiring my improvements and took exception to me being "teacher's pet". It did not occur to me that they would resent my being favoured by the tutors. Unbeknown to me, they hatched a plan to teach me a lesson, although it was not a pleasant way to learn. The next day they approached and gave me a bar of chocolate which they had bought for me. I thanked them and ate it. At the next meal there were prunes and custard, which I loved. Before I could start the dessert the girls, in an alarmed manner, told me to stop. I was surprised but they confessed that the chocolate which they had given me was a laxative and they thought I would be very ill if I added the prunes on that day, especially as I should not have eaten the whole bar. They said they had given me the laxative to remind me of my fat, rosy cheeks. They looked very sorry and kept apologising for their bad behaviour. As it happened, it did not have any serious effects. I did not tell them but managed to look somewhat poorly. I did smile sweetly and act a little coy in the presence of the Sister Tutors. I was just so pleased that they had taken a liking to me. After all, I was all alone and far from home and that made me seem brave to them. Little did they know that I was very happy to be in that situation. In order to allay their guilt, they purchased a good seat for me at the cinema. Following that incident about which I did not complain, I seemed to have become popular with the rest of the nursing school as well as with the Sister Tutors.

One advantage of being in England was that I could now communicate with my parents by letter which I had been unable to do from Israel, as Iraq would not accept any correspondence from Israel. I wrote weekly to my parents with news of my studies, experiences and friends. My father wrote back and he sent me the £14.00 air fare from Italy to England. He actually sent me £15.00 giving me £1.00 for myself! My father was not known for his generosity. I would have dearly loved a few more pounds. I was not too disappointed as I was not expecting it as far as he was concerned. I returned the money to Mr Harcourt-Samuel. My relatives in Israel were worried about what had become of me and how I would survive in a strange country like England. After I settled, I began to write to everyone and tell them how sorry I was to have departed in such a sudden, secretive manner. My days now became fun with my studies and my new friends. Weekends were free in P.T.S. and I would go to the cinema with the other girls. The cinema cost one shilling but this included two films. Some of the girls smoked and would ask me to lend them a shilling for cigarettes, but I would not give up my movie entertainment. Aunt Aggie invited me to London and sent me the train ticket as she knew that I had little money. Occasionally she would buy me clothes but I was reluctant to accept too much from her as she had already done so much for me. She was a vegetarian and we went to a vegan restaurant. We also went to the ballet and the theatre, and these were

90

amazing experiences for me. Aunt Aggie and I developed a close bond.

The P.T.S. was soon over and I commenced my nursing training in the wards and in the operating theatre. I loved meeting, caring and talking to the various patients, and I enjoyed being popular on the wards. The operating theatre was not my favourite place during my nursing career. The patients were asleep under the anaesthetic so it wasn't easy for me to understand what was happening and there was much tension all around, especially when the surgeon was stressed. The quiet atmosphere was not for me; it was hard for me to keep quiet for a long period! My favourite ward was the children's ward in Margate Hospital. I found that the children became attached to me and I would enjoy telling them stories. The sad part of the nursing was when any patients became seriously ill and died, and this was particularly so as far as the children were concerned. At times when some of the little ones were in pain, I would be reduced to tears when I returned to my room. Sometimes I would visit them on my day off and take them toys. I also had strong feelings for the elderly, especially the ones who did not have attention from their relatives. They looked so lonely at visiting times. One day I was called to the Head Sister's office and was told gently but firmly that I should not get too attached to the patients. It was not advisable in my profession. It was important to maintain a strong detached position in our relationship with the patients who relied on us.

Diana (right) during nursing training

I began to take mini-breaks with my friends or Aunt Aggie. Aunt Aggie gave me a choice as to where I would like to visit and I suggested Shakespeare's birth town. We went to Stratford-Upon-Avon and stayed in a delightful vegetarian hotel. We went to the theatre to see one of the plays, Richard III, and I felt I was dreaming. I could not believe that I was in this lovely theatre watching a Shakespearean play in Stratford-Upon-Avon. At the end of the performance I was reluctant to leave my seat. Aggie was very moved by my feelings. She laughed and said, "It is not a dream and we will return to see another play." I had been mentioning Aunt Aggie to my parents in my correspondence. I told them about the great times I had with her, so my father wrote a charming letter to her expressing his gratitude for her kindness. My father was a very good letter writer. He knew how to write in a precise and charming way. He chose his words very carefully and, of course, his English was excellent and there were definitely no spelling mistakes. Aunt Aggie was very impressed and commented how much I must have meant to him and how much he missed me. I did not disappoint her on either account.

My friend Val had become very attached to a doctor at our hospital. He was now working in London and I realised that Val wanted to see him as she was in love with him. She begged me to go with her to London for a few days' holiday and she informed her parents that I was familiar with London and I would be a very suitable person to accompany her. We found a clean and reasonable place to stay which had been recommended by a patient, and we were given special rates as we were nurses. In the daytime we would go sightseeing and Val saw her friend every evening, while I went to the cinema or visited Aunt Aggie. Val was later to marry this doctor who became a General Practitioner in Orpington. I encouraged their friendship and I still remind her how I was partly responsible for her success, although I would have a silent giggle to myself. I was like a matchmaker and I tell her that I deserve a reward. They had three sons who all became doctors and all of them worked at one time or another in the medical agency which I was later to start. Val is a very nice person who likes to help other people. She is at peace with the world and likes to view it as a happy place for everyone. She is loved by all her grandchildren and is devoted to her family. We have long conversations on the telephone reminiscing about the past. I am lucky to have her as a friend. Life is certainly strange at times and seems to write its own script. It is not an everyday occurrence to have such friendship that lasts more than half a century and involves the next generation. I went to the weddings of her two eldest sons, many years later.

I loved the countryside and I learned to ride horses. Aunt Aggie was friendly with a family of doctors who lived in the country. They were three brothers and were respectively a gynaecologist, a surgeon and an anaesthetist. They had their own clinic and lived in a lovely house. We stayed with them on several occasions and they were a happy family who welcomed me to their home. I consider myself lucky to have met such kind people and I never took their hospitality for granted. Some of the things I learnt from Aunt Aggie have been very valuable throughout my life. One in particular was to write a "Thank you" letter when people give you gifts or their hospitality, and I always did that with this family of doctors, and everyone else who had been kind to me. I taught my children this habit and I think that it is a very important thing in life to show one's appreciation to people who deserve it. It is also a good feeling when you let people know that you value their act of kindness and do not take it for granted.

In my second year, I went to a farmhouse in Cornwall with my friend Jane Seath. Her father, who ran a petrol station, treated us to the stay which included all our meals and he also gave us £5.00 each to spend; this was a large amount of money in those days. The food was fresh local farmhouse food and was excellent. Jane was an only child, like me, and we got on very well on holiday. She was the serious type so I knew not to act in my usual carefree way. I was very tempted to tease her as she was an easy target and it was in my nature to be a tease, however, I resisted. We ate lunch out every day as we made our way to the beach. Jane would have baked beans on toast whilst I would have sardines on toast. Jane disliked the look of the sardines and would bribe me not to eat them anymore. This was a big sacrifice for me considering my love of sardines! It was a lovely holiday and we both returned still good friends at the end of it.

In Ramsgate there was a Jewish religious establishment called the Judith Lady Montefiore College which had been founded by Sir Moses Montefiore in the 1880s. Occasionally I visited the college which was a training school for Rabbis and was given Matzahs at Passover. The nurses liked them and started to eat my Matzahs and I had to fight to keep enough of them for myself. One of the popular outings in Margate was to the large funfair called "Dreamland". We would go there to enjoy the many rides. However, we could not have too many rides as our money was limited.

During my nursing training, we would have to do emergency night duties in the operating theatres as well as day work, but we always had one day free every week. I was kept busy on my day off trying to catch up with all the things I needed to do such as writing letters to the family as well as one to Frère Benoit. I never started my letter to him by saying "Dear", nor did he; that was the rule. I wrote to him chiefly about all the funny things that were happening around me and my experiences on the wards. I always made it a light hearted letter and liked to think of him smiling while he was reading it. In my second year of training, I was given more responsibility and at this time I received a letter from Frère Benoit telling me that he was being promoted in the Church and that he would be coming to London to receive his elevation. He did not think that we should correspond any more but that if I ever needed his help in any way, I could feel free to contact him. Although I knew this was for the best, it was a sad day for me as our friendship was a special one which I could never replace. I went to London to the awards ceremony in Westminster. We saw each other in the distance and gave a brief wave but I did not see Frère Benoit again. On the train back to the hospital a sad feeling came over me and I could not help shedding some tears for closing a chapter in my life. Then I had to remind myself how lucky I had been to have had such a friendship. I will always remember his support and encouragement which played a large part in helping me to achieve the goals that I desired. I shall always cherish that memory. It is proof that people from entirely different backgrounds and religions can be at peace with each other and form a bond. There are many good, kind people in the world and it is a great comfort when they become part of our lives.

By my final year I was in charge of wards and supervising first year nurses. I was not too strict with these nurses as this was my nature, and they appreciated this. I found through life that such understanding produced the best results. I was able to communicate well with patients who seemed to like my accent. Patients always enjoyed our conversations and would ask me what I did on my day off and I would tell them exciting stories which were usually invented. There were various nationalities amongst the nurses but the predominant foreign contingent was the Irish. They argued frequently with the English girls about politics. The Irish girls could be very fiery and would cite, for example, the attitudes of Queen Victoria towards the Irish and other instances of British colonialism throughout the world. In a more contemporary instance the Suez crisis inspired the Irish nurses to accuse the British of more colonialism.[7] As an Israeli, I avoided the clashes so that, thankfully, I was not involved in these disputes. However, I was questioned by the Irish girls about Jerusalem. They wanted to know what the spiritual nature of that city was like. I told them that I knew Jerusalem well and that in fact on one occasion when I was staying there, I heard voices telling me that I was going to meet good people from a land beginning with "I". They all said, "That's us." I think they believed me, but certainly they were all very friendly with me and I found their company lively and cheerful.

There was an American Air Force base for fighter-bomber units near Margate called Manston. The airmen would meet nurses at a dance hall in town. Many went out together and some married and went to the U.S.A. to live, even though they knew little about their partner's background. On one occasion, there was an American Major as a patient in one of the wards. He was visited by an airman and the Major told me that this airman would like to go out with me. I agreed, after some persuasion, and he picked me up in his car and said that he would take me to his camp for dinner. After a short journey the car stopped and would not start. He seemed upset and apologetic as I did not seem to believe him. He pulled out a can of beer and started drinking. He offered me a can but I declined his offer as I did not drink. He then said he would walk to the nearest house and telephone his camp for help. I was frightened and said that I was going to get out of the car and go back to the nurses' home. It was snowing outside and he asked me how I was going to get back. I was suspicious of his intentions and got out of the car and hitched a lift back to Margate Hospital. The driver who stopped for me was one of the hospital technicians. He recognised me and made me feel uncomfortable with his opinion about girls who got impressed by the flashy American airmen. I knew that the local boys did not like having them around as far as the local girls were concerned. I explained how my date happened and that I did not know much about him and thought it best to get back to the hospital. Perhaps I misjudged the man. He wrote and apologised and said he would like to see me again, but I did not reply. I cannot even remember his name, but that was the extent of my romantic experience in my training years. I found it rather disturbing how a large number of the nurses were falling rapidly in love with the American airmen. They had no idea what they would meet when they arrived in the United States, or what security would be there for them. I suppose the glamour of the uniform and having so much money to spend had a lot to do with it, something like a holiday romance. I hope they ended up being happy and without some of the hardships that one heard about. I did not reveal my feelings to any of the girls as I had no intention of opposing cupid.

I had been using an Israeli passport of limited validity which I had renewed twice. I continued happily thinking that I would be able to keep on renewing it as long as I was doing my nursing training, but that secure feeling ended abruptly when, at the end of my second year, I received a communication from the Israeli Embassy that I should now return to Israel to join the Israel Defence Force (I.D.F.) to do my National Service. I wrote and told them that I would be pleased to do this once I had finished my nursing training, but that I did not wish to interrupt this course with only one year left before completion. I had been through a struggle with my studies for nursing and English, and to return to Israel for a period and then have to return to my nursing training and further specialisation, would have been disastrous. I was not going to let this happen and was determined to contest this interference with my career. I was going to plan everything in a calm manner and not let worries interfere with my future plans. I believed in the saying, "Fear holds you a prisoner, hope sets you free".

I was summoned to London by the Israeli authorities for a medical examination. I was given an address in Baker Street and I arrived in a nervous state. I rang the door bell at a very smart house and the door was answered immediately as if I had been expected and this made me jump. The man who answered the door reminded me of the unpleasant dentist in Baghdad whom I did not like. I asked if I could see the doctor for my medical examination. With a wide grin he said, "I am the doctor and first I have to weigh you without your clothes on." I was suspicious and he said, "Come on now you are a nurse and I am a doctor." I did not take my slip off and looked for the weighing machine. He asked me to stand and bend my elbows. I was very puzzled and suddenly he came behind me and lifted me from under my elbows and told me how much I weighed. I was stunned by what he did and showed it on my face. He laughed and announced that was the way he weighed small people. There was no one else in the room. I think he had the message that I was not amused. He was careful not to offend me with the rest of the check-up. He told me that I was a healthy girl and the Army would be pleased to have me when he sent in his report. I would have liked to have given him a kick on the shin before I left, but I had enough troubles at the time and I walked out dazed and annoyed. Two days' later I was informed that I was fit for the I.D.F., that I should return to Israel, and my passport was cancelled.

I marched to the Matron's office and told her about the request from the Israeli authorities and the struggle I had been through to get as far as I had. She was impressed and suggested I should put the whole story on paper for her. She was obviously upset to see me in such an emotional state. She said that she would make some enquiries and make a plan for me by the next day. She told me not to worry and go back to my patients with a smile and finish my shift, and this I did with a feeling of relief. In the evening I went to the nurses' sitting room with my friends. My encounter with Matron was the topic of the evening as they were all supporting me. Everyone had a theory about how Matron was going to help me. Some suggested that she had a lover in the Home Office and that pretending to be so prim in her uniform was an act and that she was a real *femme fatale*. Someone reported that she had been seen in the hospital grounds discreetly holding a man's hand. Someone else thought that she might have more than one lover as she had been taking a few days' off now and then. I told them of my experience with the doctor. They were shocked and some of the Irish nurses wanted to go to his surgery in London and strip and weigh him! That evening the girls tried to cheer me up by being jolly and light hearted. I did not sleep much that night waiting anxiously to see Matron the next day.

The next day, Matron told me that I should go to the Home Office in London. She wrote a long letter stating that I had worked very hard and was very popular with both staff and patients and that it was unfair to disrupt my training in a valuable profession. I would be able to repay the country for my training, and as a consequence I should be allowed to stay in England. It was a very impressive letter and I was allowed to read it. Meanwhile, my friends were very upset by the thought of my having to leave and were preparing to write a petition on my behalf. At the Home Office in London, I presented my case. The official behind the desk was good natured with a smiling face. It seemed that the way I presented my case touched his heart. I was having to dab my eyes a few times and was searching for a handkerchief and he almost passed me his, just like it happens in a weepy movie. I could have been nominated for an award but this was no movie, nor was this acting. I was becoming frustrated by trying to secure what was right for me. After the meeting I had a good lunch and then went back after three hours for the verdict on my case. I thought I detected a hint of a smile on the official's face. It had been a long three hours wait for me but I returned to the Home Office exactly on time.

I was given a permit to stay in the U.K, however, if I attempted to go abroad I would not be allowed to return. I was given a special document to cover my stay in the country and told that it would last until I gained my citizenship. I was told that I was a privileged young lady to have obtained such a document and I happily expressed my gratitude. Again I was met with help and kindness and, needless to say, I was greatly relieved. I celebrated by going to the cinema in London and saw "The Wizard of Oz" again. I enjoyed the magic land and felt that I was over the rainbow myself. Everyone back at the hospital was delighted at the news and my friends arranged a little party for me. Matron even gave me a hug and that was something!

During my final year, I had been considering what to do after completing my training. That was providing that I passed all my subjects in the exams. Needless to say, I was very apprehensive. I studied harder than ever, and even abandoned my trips to the cinema. As the exams approached my anxiety increased. I had to discipline myself to become calmer. My friends suggested smoking, but I would not do that. My Sister Tutors were very supportive and helped me at this time. I did not want to hear about nurses who did not pass the exams and had to re-take them, and occasionally gave up altogether. On the day of the exams I tried to be alone; I kept telling myself I had never previously failed an exam and I was not going to start now. It was about a month before the results were known and it was a worrying time for me. I volunteered for nightshifts as I was not sleeping well. On the day of the results, my friend Margaret and I decided to open each other's envelopes; we had both passed. It was an exhilarating feeling and for a while we could not take it in and then we had some tears. We jumped up and down and hugged each other. Margaret headed for home to tell her parents and I ran to the Sister Tutors to tell them the news and thanked them for their encouragement. They were waiting and expecting to hear from me. I was moved by how delighted they were to hear my news and I thought I saw a sign of tears in their eyes. They gave me a big hug and I thought they must have felt proud at what they had accomplished with me. At the nurses' home we could not have a party as some of our set did not pass. I celebrated in my usual way by going to the cinema, accompanied by some of the other girls. I wrote to my parents to tell them that I had been successful in all my exams and about the help given to me by the tutors. I received a letter back saying they were very proud of me and that they were going to try to get out of Baghdad and come to England. They would like to then continue their journey to Israel with me. I had no plans to accompany them for the time being, but I thought I would bide my time to tell them that when and if they arrived here.

Having passed the exams I rather liked the idea of midwifery. There were no midwifery schools in Margate and Ramsgate and so I decided to apply to London where I really wished to go. I was accepted for midwifery training in East London, and before I left Margate I worked as a staff nurse for about three months taking responsibility for a ward when the Sister was not on duty. I needed some money before I went to London. I had cut my own hair and my friends admired my work and so I offered to cut all the girls' hair for payment. When I had finished it was remarked that all the nurses looked alike as they all had the same hair style! I also had a jumble sale of my old clothes and then I said my farewells to my friends, who gave me a party and a present of a Turner print. It was an emotional occasion after three and a half interesting and happy years. Having to say goodbye was not easy. I knew that I would see some of my friends again, but not all of them. I had to say goodbye to Matron who told me how pleased she was for me and how different I looked now compared to the scared girl I had been when I arrived. Her parting words were, "Have compassion in life and with that you will not go wrong." It was hard to say goodbye to my Sister Tutors but I promised to keep in touch and visit them, which I did.

From the time I arrived in England I can say that I had not encountered hostility of any kind. I loved the way I was received and to me it has become my adopted country. I still love Israel and look forward to visiting as often as I can in the future. It will always have a special place in my heart. I have been blessed, here in England, by being surrounded by very kind people which made me feel that I belonged. I have never taken anything for granted. I have worked hard to accomplish my goals as I wanted a respected position in society. Because I have been so lucky, I have always had the desire to repay this kindness to others whenever possible. Although over the years I have travelled and seen many new places, I am always glad to come back home, which is England for me. Sometimes I wonder what it would be like to go back to where I lived in Baghdad and see my old school again and what it would be like to see my house and discover if it has changed. I would like to walk to the ice cream parlour where they sold the best ice cream I ever tasted. I addressed the ice cream vendor as "Sir" and always thanked him sweetly with a smile so that he would give me a little extra, although my cousins did not approve of my insincere flattery. I try to remember all the things that are pleasant and how lovely it would be if there was peace in the world and people could go wherever they wished. However, these memories are like dreams and when you wake they are gone.

TWELVE

London

I travelled by train to London with my few possessions and went directly to Plaistow Maternity Hospital in East London. I reported to the office and was shown to my room in an old and gloomy building. There were ten of us starting the midwifery course and we all had the required State Registered Nursing Certificates. The course was one year divided into Parts 1 and 2, each of six months. The teaching was intensive and I spent some time in the delivery rooms and also visiting women who wanted to have their babies at home, accompanied by a trained midwife. The area was very impoverished; sometimes it was very upsetting to see how some people lived, especially families with many children in a small and confined dwelling. I had not encountered this side of life before. I did not make any particular friends on the course, but one of the expectant mothers had a small boy who was keen on football. He was very sweet and polite. His father was in the Navy and was away at sea much of the time. When at home, his father frequented the pubs and we were told by his wife that he had no time for the little boy. When I next saw the boy I promised him that I would take him to a football match and his little face lit up. It was a rough area and so one of the doctors, who was treating his mother and who was a great football fan, accompanied me and the boy to watch West Ham football team play. It was a pleasure to see how he enjoyed himself and the three of us went a few more times; I still like football to this day. The boy, the doctor and I developed a happy friendship so we were all upset when the time came to say goodbye. "Goodbye" is a word that should be abolished in all languages. I seemed to be using it a lot and I cannot say that I enjoyed doing that. I realised, as I was coming to the end of my first six months, that midwifery was not for me and I decided to leave without completing the full course. This was one of the very few occasions that I said, "Goodbye," with pleasure to the Sister in charge of the Unit who we had named "Sister Battleaxe". She managed to make some of the girls cry with her criticisms. Her advice to me before I left was, "Toughen up if you want to aim high in your nursing career." My reply was that I could never be unnecessarily tough or unapproachable in order to establish my authority. This was not needed if respect has been earned previously. It would also lead to loneliness and I don't like being alone. At that, I bid my farewell. I had a pleasant feeling after that and hoped that she would give a thought to what I had said.

I found a temporary Staff Nurse position at the National Temperance Hospital in Central London and I moved into the nurses' accommodation. This was an ideal location for me as I had all the cinemas nearby and, in addition, there were free tickets given to the nurses for many of the London theatre performances. I was put to work on the private ward. Looking back on that particular period there was something unusual happening. Gary, my future husband, was doing a short locum at the same hospital at that time, but our paths never crossed. It was odd but then fate plays funny games.

I was still in touch with my old friends in Margate and one day four of them came to visit and they all stayed the night in my room. I met many interesting patients while at the National Temperance Hospital, including Eric Boon who was an English boxing title holder at Lightweight. One of my patients was a film critic and he gave me tickets to watch films and to give him my views. I would see three films in a day when I was off duty, and report back to him. This was great fun for me. I made two new friends at the National Temperance Hospital: Dorie who came from the North of England and was very pretty and the girlfriend of Eric Boon, and Suzy who came from Iraq; so sometimes we were able to speak together in Arabic. Suzy was a volatile girl who spoke in a loud voice and liked to complain about the English weather, although she would not have liked to return to Iraq. She had two sisters in London and they were all Christians and were not comfortable with the regime in Iraq.

During my period of working at the National Temperance Hospital, I had an unusual experience. In my capacity as a Staff Nurse I was at times in charge of the private ward and the children's ward which were situated next to each other. I had the help of some Assistant Nurses who were very capable. I loved being on the children's ward except when one of them was seriously ill and I would become upset. The children enjoyed my games and playing funny tricks on them. Before bedtime I used to tell them a funny story that I made up. They preferred that to me reading from a book. One night just as I was about to begin a story, I was summoned to the private ward where one of the patients who had been with us for a while was not feeling well. He was 90 years old and had been very alert until then and he liked having a conversation with me. He did not seem to be too distressed and I had a short talk with him and told him how I entertained the children. He told me to carry on with the children and I said I would see him shortly. One of the children on the ward lost a tooth and I told him to put it under his pillow and the tooth fairy would put something there for him. I intended to do so myself and returned to the private ward but, unfortunately, my friendly patient had passed away. He was then prepared in the customary fashion and put on a trolley. I wanted to wheel the trolley to the mortuary with the porter. I thought it was my way of saying "Goodbye." Now the porter that night was an Italian who liked to exhibit his masculinity, he did not like women giving him orders. I had a feeling he did not like me, especially when I told him to push the trolley carefully. He mumbled that he was being pushed around with too many orders and he was very busy that night. I said OK he could go as soon as we got inside the mortuary and that I would position the trolley in the correct place. I had the keys to the mortuary door and as soon as the door opened and we got inside, he left very speedily. He obviously did not like the mortuary. It was a frightening experience when I heard the heavy door slam behind him. I thought this could not be happening to me. Was I dreaming that I was here with all the dead bodies and I had left the key in the door? It was very cold and I was feeling increasingly uncomfortable. I banged on the door and shouted for help but there was no one to hear me as the mortuary was outside the main building. In having to deal with the porter, I had forgotten to keep the keys with me and I even wondered whether he had closed the door on purpose. I was talking to myself as there was no one to answer me and hoping that someone would notice my absence on the wards and remember me leaving with the porter. As I looked around I had a horribly sad feeling. I could not converse with anyone; each of them must have had a story to tell. I wondered what kind of life each of them had led and I hoped that they had enjoyed a happy life. I suddenly wasn't frightened and I felt at peace. In order to keep myself occupied I started to tell them my life story. Afterwards, I kept thinking what it must be like to live one's life in the same location and in a straight forward manner without any difficulties. That was a happy thought.

The little boy with the lost tooth woke up crying that there was no present under his pillow as the nurse had promised. The nurses said that they would look for me and see what had happened about the tooth fairy. So the search began and the porter was asked where I was. He had to admit that he left me in the mortuary on my own at my request, and he thought that I had the keys with me but added that they might still be in the door. I think he said that reluctantly. I was beginning to get very distressed and cold; there was nowhere to sit and I started running around to keep warm. It was like something out of a horror movie. I would have even been pleased to meet Count Dracula in order to speak to someone! I could not believe it when I heard cries outside the door saying, "We are here." My hands were very cold and painful from banging on the door, but I was delighted to be liberated, and although it had not been so long it seemed to me to have been hours. I was not even annoyed about the porter any more although, in fact, he left the hospital a few days later. The nurse told me that the search began after my little patient had asked for me. The nurses made a fuss of me and I went home before my shift finished. The first thing I did the next day was to buy a gift "From the tooth fairy" for my little friend. I thought after my ordeal that Matron would recommend me for an O.B.E., or something, but all I got was "Well done Staff Nurse." I suppose that is what they would have put on my tomb stone if I had not been rescued. It would not have been like me to let such an unusual event pass without spreading all the details around the hospital. Of course, I added a little extra to it. I even began to think of charging a fee each time I repeated it! When I wrote to my cousins informing them what had happened to me they refused to believe or accept my story because of my history of storytelling. As far as my parents were concerned, they trembled with fear just reading my letter.

I stayed in the nurses' quarters at the National Temperance Hospital for a few months and was then persuaded by Suzy to rent a room in the house in Devonshire Street where she was staying. The house was owned by an Egyptian lady who was said to be a princess, but she was certainly from a high society background. Devonshire Street is one of the prestigious streets in London. Some well known celebrities live there. There were five of us girls and we shared a communal lounge and kitchen. The rent was high and it left me little money from my salary, but the location in Central London made it worthwhile. Before taking up residence, I decided to have a break from work. I had received a refund from some overpaid National Insurance contributions and I found a bed and breakfast guest house in Bournemouth, Southern England, where I stayed for ten days. I had heard about this seaside resort and I was lucky to have good weather throughout my stay. I sunbathed on the beach and went to the cinema every day. Little did I know that one day I would be living in this town with my children and grandchildren. Leaving Bournemouth after my ten day break, I could not guess that the next time I would be there would be on my honeymoon.

On my return to London, I moved into the room in Devonshire Street which was off Portland Place and near Regent's Park. All the residents were girls and were mainly secretaries, apart from Suzy, myself and one other nurse called Pari who was from Iran and was of the Bahai faith. I became friendly with several of the girls including Anne and Dina.

At this time I found work as a Staff Nurse at a branch of the National Hospital for Nervous Diseases in Soho through a nursing agency. The work was not too strenuous and I was certainly in the middle of cosmopolitan London. Suzy liked to arrange parties in the house in Devonshire Street. Pari was getting engaged to a doctor and Suzy decided that we should throw a party to celebrate the occasion. Suzy collected contributions and gave me money to buy cheeses, bread and other items for the snacks. Dina who was from India and was a Zoroastrian, went with me to the shops. Neither of us was keen on Suzy's parties and finding a film we wished to see, and having some money for once in my pocket, we went to a cinema in Baker Street without purchasing any snacks. I did give my action a good deal of thought as I didn't think that I would have the courage to go through with it. I don't recall having done such a dishonest thing as this before. Dina's opinion was that there was plenty of food in the house and no shortage of drink. In any case, we would return the money on pay day. Needless to say, I didn't need much persuasion to continue with what we had planned. I did feel rather guilty but the film was very good, it was called "Green for Danger". We stayed out as late as possible as I was apprehensive about facing Suzy, although I had an apology ready. We returned to the house very late in the evening hoping that the party in the common lounge would have ended and that Suzy would not be too angry or had gone to bed, but that was not to be. She was too busy to confront me but gave me a look that said I will deal with you later. In the event, the party was not over and as I entered the room a man came across to talk to me. I noticed he had been in conversation with Suzy just as I was entering the room. Apparently, Gary asked her, "Who is that girl?" Her reply was that I was the nasty flat mate who took her money.

She ignored me for the rest of the evening. I stepped back for a moment and as he drew near I said to him, "I am Jewish." He replied, "So am I." I then asked him, "Are you a doctor?" I knew that most of the guests were doctors. He replied, "Yes I am." I then said, "Are you British?" he said with a smile, "Yes." I then asked him if he had a British passport. He answered in the affirmative. According to my husband to be, Gary, I then asked him if he would like to come to the cinema with me the next evening. The latter part of the conversation only took place in Gary's imagination. He seems to have captured audiences with this story and it seems to keep him happy as his story has been repeated through the years and has never failed to amuse people at dinner parties. I even began to enjoy and believe it so I never corrected him and that is why I am relating it here. That was the start of my relationship with Gary. Suzy had said that if I did not go dancing with her I would never meet a man. I replied that one day someone would appear on my doorstep and I was proved right. Accordingly, the next evening we met in Leicester Square and went to see a film. It starred Henry Fonda but the title now escapes me. I did not encourage or flirt with him straight away because Suzy had accused me in the past of flirting with her boyfriends after which she never saw them again. That was all in her imagination, she hardly ever had any boyfriends and when she did they were not worth flirting with. I was never offended by Suzy and still like her a lot. I must say it was a pleasant surprise when I discovered Suzy's approval of my relationship with Gary. I had to remind her about my saying about finding someone at my doorstep as a potential boyfriend and how lucky she was that we had not bet on it. We had a good laugh at that.

Gary was a Houseman in a hospital in East London and we started to go out in the evenings when neither of us was on duty. At weekends we visited various places around London. Gary's school friend Ken and his wife Anna Maria were in London at that time and we went out together to places of interest such as the zoo. Gary took me to Kew Gardens and Richmond where we ate at a lovely hotel, and I appreciated Gary's generosity. One of the most important qualities I look for in a man is generosity. Without it life can be unpleasant. If only my father had had that quality, his life would have been enriched and a happy one. I am pleased to say that it was certainly one of my mother's qualities. I have a clear memory of the street sweeper who was a single father with two sons. My mother would give the three of them food on most days as well as some pocket money. This was all done before my father got home and we never mentioned it to him. I knew why without having to ask her as my father did not have the same values about life. It was touching to see the look of content on their faces, especially when she handed them a parcel of food to take home for the weekend. I used to have to fight a happy tear in my eyes and I thought very highly of my mother. I wished that she could have opened her arms to me for a hug so that I could tell her that I loved her. However, such a display of affection was not going to happen. Instead I just stood at the window and waved goodbye to the street sweeper and his sons.

I received a letter from my cousin Daisy. She had married and emigrated from Israel to New York. Her husband was a successful businessman and he was able to help her parents who had remained in Israel. Daisy and I were always in contact. She informed me that she knew a dentist in New York who was very wealthy. He was a Jewish Iraqi and was looking for a wife. She told me that I would be "dripping in gold" if I married him. I replied and told her that, much as I would like to be weighed down with gold nuggets, I was happy in England at present, although the idea of going to the United States appealed to me and I wrote and told her so.

Gary had arranged to go to sea as a ship's doctor travelling to Australia on a P & O Liner for a few months. That arrangement was made before we met. By the time he was due to leave, I had become friendly with his mother as we had some things in common, our fondness of movies and good food. He gave me a list of the ports and the dates he would be arriving at them, and I sent him postcards to the ship at these locations. Our correspondence was of a humorous nature and did not involve mushy love letters. I still have some of these amusing postcards. At the time of Gary's departure I was working at the West End Hospital for Nervous Diseases in Soho. I decided to do mostly night duty. I liked the peace and quiet of the night especially if there were no emergencies. Most of the patients slept well as they were on sedative medications. I would enjoy chatting to them before I put the lights out. A nursing sister in the hospital was from India. She had children who were musicians and who travelled around the country giving concerts. When she heard that I could do belly-dancing she asked me if I would like to travel to a concert in Manchester. I agreed, and we all went together and I danced on stage to the accompaniment of Indian music. However, it was not the belly dancing that I did. I did not like doing that in front of a big audience full of strangers. So far, it had been reserved for family gatherings. Reluctantly they allowed me to change my routine and join three girls and two boys doing a charming little song and dance number which was a success. I enjoyed the experience, but I did not repeat it. I also decided that was not the door into show business. In fact, I had potential to be a movie star and with that imaginary thought I continued to have sweet dreams whilst performing my every day routine.

THIRTEEN

Moorfield's Eye Hospital

I was always interested in how eyes worked and thought that it must be devastating to have something wrong with your eyes preventing you from reading, especially where reading was an extremely important part of one's life. I just could not imagine life without being able to read. One day, my eyes felt tired and I thought a little blurred. I panicked, rushed to the chemist and bought a large bottle of Optrex. The chemist who served me could see that I was upset and he asked me why I had such a gloomy face on such a nice spring day and why I needed such a large amount of Optrex? I told him not to worry as I was not intending to take my life with Optrex. He gave a big laugh and said that it would be difficult as Optrex was only purified water. I explained that I wanted to keep washing my eyes so that I could read clearly. However, I was able to see everything around me. He took the Optrex back and told me that I should see an optician as I might need glasses. He also gave me a small container of soothing drops and asked me to return and tell him if the drops had helped; he also gave me the address of a good optician. Eyes are very precious he concluded, and I left his shop feeling much happier. Next day I saw an optician and was told that my eyes were in good order, but if I was reading a lot I needed some glasses but not particularly strong ones. I celebrated this good news with a visit to the cinema!

The thought of knowing more about eyes didn't leave me. I had heard a lot about Moorfield's Eye Hospital in London which was considered to be one of the foremost hospitals in that speciality, and it was not far from where I lived. I was told by the Matron of the hospital where I was working that it was difficult to get into Moorfield's, but she was willing to write me a good reference, not that I deserved it, she said with a wink! She added she would be sorry to lose me if I was successful. I completed all the necessary forms for a post-graduate course at Moorfield's and waited. I went back to the helpful chemist to thank him and keep him posted with all my news. Proudly I presented him with the best box of chocolates I could afford. He gave me a big smile and thanked me, but declined the chocolates as he suffered from diabetes. I thought of a very good use for that box of chocolates. I presented it to the staff where I worked as a departing gesture for the lovely bunch of girls I had worked with. They were delighted and I enjoyed pleasing them all. It was a while before I got a reply from Moorfield's Hospital. I was very apprehensive when the envelope arrived as I had already broadcasted to so many people about my application which was foolish as I would be humiliated if I did not get in, but I even thought of leaving town and then I remembered the famous film star, John Wayne, who never ran away from problems but just faced them. So, with that thought, I opened the letter and to my delight I had been accepted and was due to start the following month. I informed my Matron and thanked her for my reference, but I did wonder whether it was her way of getting rid of me! Her reply was that she was hoping I wouldn't guess, followed by one of her winks. There was a lady who knew how to be a human being and will always be respected without having to impose her authority. I have always learned from people who showed me the good quality of their nature. Perhaps I will end my conversations in future with a wink.

The first day of starting my new post I was very excited; I had not read the instructions carefully and I am hopeless at finding my way around. I usually got lost going home and I knew there was a Moorfield's Hospital in the City and I headed there. When I arrived I gave my name and State Registered Nurse registration number. They seemed to be very pleased to see me. I was given a uniform and the names of a few patients that I had to look after. I was very confused, I thought it a strange way of giving a student such responsibility, and I thought that the hospital was very small to be so famous. I was rather disappointed but I walked to the first patient and stood there not knowing what to do. He seemed to sense my uncertainty; I told him that I was not an eye nurse but just a student and I was supposed to be having a lecture today but they seemed to be so busy and that I did not have time to discuss any arrangements with them. The patient was pleased and told me what to do and hoped that changing the dressings would not be so rough as it had sometimes been. I did not treat anyone else. I looked round and suddenly saw a sign that said, "Moorfield's Hospital, City Branch". It was so embarrassing that I could have made such a mistake but, at the same time, I was relieved. I went to the Head Sister and explained that I was only a student and was supposed to be at the Moorfield's branch at High Holborn. She was not amused; I kept apologising about the mistake and explained about the patient I had treated with his help! I stood there while she looked at me with distaste. Mistakes did not exist in her dictionary. She certainly wasn't one of the most understanding people I had met. To make people feel small is not an achievement. I feel sorry for people like her who miss out on happiness. Happiness is like a butterfly, it won't land on one shoulder if you don't let it. I suppose you cannot win them all! I left the place in a hurry and reached the correct destination as quickly as I could. I was very impressed with the hospital as it was a lovely building in the middle of the hustle and bustle of London, and I went straight to Matron's office and explained what had happened, and apologised. To my amazement she thought it was rather funny. She briefed me as to what was going to happen. There were six of us on the course, with one who was arriving from Ireland the next day. That day, I was to get acquainted with the place and find my way around. She said that with a hint of a smile. I wondered whether she was thinking about what had happened today. I was almost tempted to say that this time I would follow the yellow brick road but, of course, I didn't tempt my luck just because she was so nice. I thanked her and walked away politely. My way of thanking would be to become a good eye nurse.

The other girls on the course arrived the next day; one of them was an Irish girl call Oona. They were all friendly but apart from Oona, they were very serious. Oona and I got on very well straight away. We had lectures on certain days of the week and worked on the wards for much of the time with supervision for certain cases. Oona and I made a good team when we were on duty together. We shared the same sense of humour as well as a love of the cinema. It was great to be part of the team in that hospital. I did not take my responsibilities lightly. The atmosphere among the patients was a cheerful one as they were not usually in physical pain and this helped the nurses to be relaxed. Some of the patients had covers over their eyes to avoid any straining and some had to be fed to avoid much movement. The meals always consisted of very soft food such as minced meat and mashed potatoes. When asked,

"What's for lunch nurse?" as I approached a patient I would say that it was a delicious, juicy steak with all the trimmings. After a while the patients began to understand me and they would announce that if it was steak again they would sooner have mince and mashed potatoes. That ended my comedy act. I had, in fact, noticed that some of the patients were whispering to each other so I guess it was their plot to deal with my nonsense. I found that the patients out-smarting me an enjoyable episode and I admitted my defeat in good spirit. I was rewarded with a little applause.

Once we had a large man who was an Irish labourer as a patient. He was a great character with a big smile on his face. But the smile faded when he used to see Oona and me marching up to him. We marched with military precision with all the right weapons lying on the trolley that we wheeled towards him. He knew what was coming (blanket bath time). He would groan, "Oh not again." We insisted that it was our duty to keep him clean and refreshed and we added with a little grin that we might repeat the performance at the end of the day. He said that he was worried in case his mother would not recognise him if he got any cleaner. He also looked forward to our day off as other kind nurses did not insist on his cleanliness.

There was a patient on the ward who once, many years ago, was a ship's captain. He was elderly and very forgetful, but most of the time he thought he was still in command of the ship. We made him happy by pretending we were part of the crew and before mealtimes he would call to us for his drink. We would give him a glass of juice and he would be displeased with the barman for such a weak drink. When he was due to be discharged his son came to collect him. I told him about our little game with his father and he laughed and was pleased with the good effect it had on his father as he now seemed to be contented. He added that he would continue with the same game and perhaps reinforce it somewhat. We said goodbye to the captain and I missed being called steward. I think that keeping the patients happy helps to speed their recovery, although this can be hard to accomplish when things get too busy.

Another patient who used to be a stand-up comedian entertaining in pubs and small theatrical venues liked playing tricks on the nurses especially me and Oona. As his health was improving Oona and I informed him that we would be able to take him to the main bathroom instead of his blanket baths. We both smiled at him and he said he didn't like the mischievous looks on our faces. We assured him that he would be getting top treatment as he was a celebrity. The day arrived when he was due for his bath. On his way there we marched on either side of him while he was telling the other patients how lucky he was to be taken to be washed by two lovely nurses. After helping him out of the bath we informed him that we were leaving him now to stand up and drip dry. He had a shocked look on his face and we told him that if he insisted on a towel we would get him one. Of course he did want a towel and Oona came in with a very small hand towel whereupon he burst out laughing and told us that we had potential to be comediennes and that he would happily consider us for a part in his act. We said we could not do that because we liked him and would not want to be a threat to his career.

Oona fell for one of the doctors whom she found very attractive. If he called for help she would be there in a flash. I was told to stand near her in case she fainted if he was friendly or smiled at her. Oona's romantic dreams turned into a nightmare after she caught a glimpse of him having a quick kiss with another nurse in the linen cupboard. She almost fainted then but couldn't because I wasn't there to catch her! She described it as a scene from a horror movie. From that time, Oona was not keen to assist that doctor and I would help him instead. After some days he enquired if she was all right as she did not seem herself. I informed him that she had seen a horror movie which had upset her a great deal and the star of the movie had a considerable resemblance to him and perhaps that was why she was avoiding him. He looked very puzzled and raised his eyebrows and said that he would have to see that movie. At that, I made a quick departure saying I was needed elsewhere as he was about to ask the name of the film. I suppose I could have called it "The Linen Cupboard Tragedy". I did manage to get Oona to laugh at my story. However, she drowned her sorrows by falling in love with the Head of Finance for the hospital when she went to enquire about an error in her pay slip. So it was a happy ending to this episode. I thought that Oona would be heading for a few more episodes of falling in love. There seemed to be lots of "Mr Right" as far as she was concerned, that was part of her sweet and trusting nature.

My course at Moorfields soon came to an end. I had enjoyed my time there but both Oona and I had to move on. Oona returned to Ireland and I never saw her again. Needless to say, I missed her a lot. It wouldn't have been the same for her as she was one of six children, although she wrote and said that she missed me too. We were a good comedy act. I did invite her to my wedding but she could not come. We lost touch shortly after that letter, writing obviously was not one of our strong points, but the memory of our short friendship will not fade away. I never found out if Oona found, "Mr Right."

*

Whilst Gary was at sea I went out several times with his mother. She had been left a widow in her forties. Gary's father, Nathaniel, was a dentist who came originally from South Africa. He was sent to study at a boarding school in England at the age of seven when his mother died in childbirth. She had been educated in England and wished that her children would also be educated there. Gary's father qualified as a dentist at Guy's Hospital Dental School. He was a very kind and caring man but, unfortunately, I never had a chance to meet him. He wanted Gary to study medicine and was very pleased when Gary gained a place at St. Mary's Hospital Medical School. It was a sunny Sunday in the summer when Gary's father collapsed in the garden and had a fatal heart attack at the age of fifty-three. It was a severe shock for both Gary and his mother who were devastated. It was very sad that Gary's father never saw him qualify as a doctor. Gary's father was never in the habit of taking Gary a cup of tea early on a Sunday morning, however, that day he did just before he collapsed. Apparently, Gary's mother was surprised by his action. How strange, was it sixth sense to see the son he loved very dearly without knowing it would be the last time that he saw him? As I write these lines I cannot stop myself from being tearful.

On the return journey from Australia, Gary decided to leave the ship. He told me he would like to go to Australia to work as a General Practitioner (G.P.), so he found an obstetric post in Woolwich, London, to gain experience in that field before travelling abroad. We continued to see each other regularly. Our relationship was a happy one and Gary's family welcomed me, making me feel comfortable in their homes. The fact that I was all alone in the country and the background of my story made them want to make me feel wanted. I also grew very fond of his uncles and aunts.

I had been finding that the lady who managed the house in Devonshire Street was difficult to deal with and the atmosphere with the other girls was no longer so cheerful, so I decided to move and found a room in a house in Belsize Park. The house was full of a variety of characters. One was an aspiring actor who was always awaiting a call on the communal telephone to receive an offer to audition; his preference was for boyfriends. There was a photographer in the building and one day I noticed a hole had been bored in the door of the bathroom and I suspected the photographer was using this to take some interesting photos. When I told Johnny, the actor, about this he exclaimed how dreadful for the girls, but I told him that it was probably meant for him. He said, "What a filthy beast." Miss Brody who lived on an upper floor always took the wrong 'phone messages. Johnny would ring in to see if there were any messages for him and Miss Brody would answer and say that Johnny was not in. It was very difficult to convince Miss Brody that it was actually Johnny speaking. In practice, Miss Brody probably had a negative effect on Johnny's career. Another resident was Ray. He was depressed most of the time, even when he had no reason to be depressed. He would ask me to lend him a shilling for his gas meter so that he could commit suicide, but the next day I would find him still alive but wanting to borrow another shilling, presumably for another suicide attempt. This pattern carried on for a while until I told Ray that I could not finance his suicide attempts anymore, so he had better cease them.

Before I left Devonshire Street the lady who collected the rents suggested that I should apply to be an air hostess with B.O.A.C. This was a very famous airline and it was very hard to obtain such a post. She was very willing to help me fill in the application and to prepare a C.V. for me. She thought that it would look good on the C.V. that I was a nurse and could speak three languages. She completed the application, enclosed a picture of me and sent it off. I received a letter informing me that I should attend a preliminary interview in the City. I went there and was told to wait for my main interview at Heathrow Airport. I was not hopeful and was not worried about being successful. Eventually, I received a letter saying I had been selected for interview. The lady who had helped me was more excited than I was. I had met a girl called Clare at the preliminary interview and she had told me that she had a car and would be driving to the airport so that if we both got selected and I did not have transport it would be a good idea to travel together and share the expense. We exchanged telephone numbers and she called to say that she was very excited to also have been chosen to attend at Heathrow Airport. The following week we travelled together and she was surprised that I was not nervous at all. I told her that it was due to a deficiency in my nervous system. It was meant to be a joke but she took it seriously. There were eight of us to be interviewed, I was number seven and Clare was number eight. She became agitated to be the last. When my turn came I entered the room to face the panel which consisted of four men and two women. They were all very pleasant and made me feel at ease. A smile goes a long way on such occasions to relieve the tension. I was asked a number of questions and they seemed to be interested in how I ended up where I now was. I did my best to be brief as I was sure that was the right way to behave. I expressed my feelings of interest in meeting passengers of different nationalities and to do my best in serving them and making their journey a happy one. I thought they were rather impressed with my little speech. I was then asked for my passport. I produced my expired Israeli passport and my English document which was like an I.D. They looked disappointed and were sorry to explain that I could not land in an Arab country with an Israeli passport even if it was now expired and many B.O.A.C. destinations were in these countries. They explained that without a British passport I would not be able to fly with them. After that there was an uneasy feeling on both sides, but I assured them that I understood. I was told to apply again when I acquired British citizenship. They asked me what was my next move and I assured them that I was going to continue with my present nursing job which I enjoyed very much. I thanked them and bid them goodbye. Clare, my nervous friend, saw me smiling and she thought I had been selected. I told her that I would wait for her. It did not seem to be a long wait and she came out very upset. We headed for the car and as we sat down I understood through her tears that she was not selected as she was not suitable material. She found this kind of rejection hurtful and she was not looking forward to facing her two flat mates who were both air hostesses. She could not understand how I was taking my rejection so calmly. I didn't like to explain why I had failed to get the job. I just shrugged and said nothing. She kept saying that it was unfair. I did my best to comfort her as I was worried about her driving in that state. Eventually she calmed down after producing several bars of Kit Kat which she started to eat in succession forgetting to offer me any. We proceeded on our way home. It was heavy traffic so she could not drive fast or do any erratic driving but she kept banging the wheel at the traffic lights. It was a relief and a happy moment for me when our journey ended. I thanked her and paid my share of the costs. I bid her goodbye and meant it. This was one of the occasions when I enjoyed using that word.

Diana in Paris, before her engagement to Gary

Gary was finishing his obstetric appointment and had been informed by an Australian doctor that if he wished to go into General Practice in Australia, knowledge of anaesthetics would be helpful. He accordingly replied to an advertisement at his teaching hospital in London and was given a Senior House Officer post in anaesthetics for six months.

I then heard that my father had suffered a small stroke. My mother and father were not given permission to leave Iraq but Gary managed to obtain an invitation for a medical assessment of my father by a top London Neurologist and this enabled them to leave Iraq. They arrived at Heathrow Airport with their few possessions and Gary and I went to meet them. It was a strange feeling; the last time I had seen them was almost thirteen years ago when they were fast asleep. I was apprehensive as to how to greet them. I had been through so much and my old life now seemed like a dream, and this made me feel distant. Although I felt sorry for them, I could not say that I was too emotional about the reunion. There was not much hugging or kissing as none of us had been used to that in the past. All kinds of feelings came flooding back from the past but I did not allow myself any resentment. I found an apartment for them near me in Belsize Park. They were both miserable and despite getting away from Baghdad, they had left almost everything, including their house, behind. They found it difficult to adjust to the new environment. The plan was that they would proceed to Israel after arrangements had been made for them. My Uncle Sassoon had some of my father's money there already and some associates of my father had a little money for him in England, but altogether they left Baghdad with very little.

During his anaesthetic appointment Gary proposed and we got engaged. I was waiting one night for him in his room at St.

127

Mary's Hospital to go out. He was supposed to finish at eight p.m. but he didn't arrive until midnight and I had fallen asleep in the chair. When I awoke Gary was standing there looking very tired but smiling. I asked him if he thought he was the charming prince and I was the sleeping beauty. He replied, "Yes that is correct," and would I marry him. Soon after he received a letter informing him that he had been appointed for a further six months' post in anaesthetics and finding that he was enjoying the work decided to make this his career choice and abandon the idea of General Practice. We had, in fact, been offered a one-way passage to Australia with Gary acting as a ship's doctor on a cargo ship of the Port Line, and me acting as a nurse, but Gary turned the offer down. The news of my engagement to Gary was not received by my parents with hearty congratulations or signs of being pleased for my future happiness. I think that they still retained the thought that I might abandon everything to be with them. It was hurtful but it did not come as a surprise. They still thought that they were perfect parents and would never admit to the fact that they had not tried very hard to see me for thirteen years. They were just two weak characters and I could not be angry with them or confront them about how I had felt throughout the years. If I had done so, they would have just crumbled and in my own way I still loved them and had no intention of making them unhappy. I have always thought that to be bitter and self-pitying is very unhealthy. As the saying goes, "To understand all is to forgive all." I explained to them in a gentle way why I could not throw away everything I had worked for and join them. I was sure that they would like to see me happy. We would be able to see each other as often as possible and they would be with all the family in Israel. I seemed to manage to cheer them up as much as it was possible. They let me understand that they were proud and pleased for me. They wished to leave England as soon as possible as the climate was not agreeing with them and there was no mention of my forthcoming wedding.

My parents proceeded with their plan to go to Israel where they both had siblings. My father went to the Israeli Agency in London and was granted permission for them both to make "Aliyah" i.e. to become Israeli citizens. The right to return was given to all Jews, and support for their travel and subsequent settlement in Israel was given to my parents. They were met by my Uncle Sassoon and in a short while he found them a small apartment which they could just afford. My father wrote and told me that their apartment overlooked a kindergarten and he did not like the noise. I remembered that my father had never liked children or the noise they made, so it was ironic that they should end up in such close proximity to them. They also wanted to let me know they were happy with my choice of a husband as they had grown to know Gary while in England, and they were eagerly waiting for us to visit them. With her experience of sewing, my mother managed to find a job in a shop owned by a lady from Baghdad. She had a big family and in a short while they made my mother feel one of them. The shop was attached to their house which suited my mother as she could rest if she needed to. This was the first time in her life that she had worked. I understood from my father's letters that she loved her work and that made me happy. I also came to hear that from her meagre salary she would buy fish for Uncle Nassim, her brother, which he liked and could not afford. I was very touched because that was the side of my mother that I always liked, being the giver.

Gary and I were now planning our wedding. Between us we saved up for the reception. We were married in an

Orthodox synagogue in North London, near to my mother-in-law's home, in February 1962. The reception was at a nearby hall and amongst the guests was, of course, Aunt Aggie. Johnny, the actor, gave an excellent humorous speech. Gary employed two medical students as bar men and their liberality in serving the drinks ensured a lively occasion. My parents were not present at my wedding; they did not feel that they could cope with meeting so many strangers and my mother not being able to speak a word of English. I was rather sad but I did not let it show. Apart from family, the guests were mainly medical and nursing friends. We went on honeymoon to Bournemouth and this time I stayed in a smart hotel. On our return, we lived for a while with my mother-in-law. It was hard for me to adjust to living in someone else's house after being independent for such a long time.

FOURTEEN

Boston, Massachusetts

Gary was now working as a Registrar in a North London Hospital and I was a Staff Nurse in the Casualty Department of a nearby hospital. His colleagues were from several different countries, including Malaysia, Australia, India and Pakistan as well as the British Isles, and we all had a lively social life. We were now living in a flat in Winchmore Hill and at this time I was pregnant with our first child. Gary commenced his studies for the higher speciality exams. A year abroad was commonly undertaken by doctors who were specialising, and following an interview in London with the Professor of the Department of Anaesthetics, he was given the post of Clinical Fellow in Anaesthesia at Massachusetts General Hospital in Boston, U.S.A. for one year, but with an option to stay longer. This was the main teaching hospital for Harvard Medical School students. As a result of this offer, we were given our American visas and green cards without any difficulty. Gary had now abandoned the idea of going to Australia as we both thought it would be too far away. I loved the thought of going to the United States so that I could be near my cousins and see them again after such a long time. I was longing to see New York but I knew that I would miss London and Gary's family that I had come to love. I reassured my mother-in-law that should we decide to stay in America we would certainly be happy for her to join us. Meanwhile, we had to wait for our baby's arrival before we travelled.

Our first child, Jonathan, was born in April 1963 in the British Hospital for Mothers and Babies at Woolwich, where Gary had worked up to three months prior to our departure on the Holland America liner "Rotterdam". Arriving in New York I went to stay with my cousin Daisy, while Gary went to Boston and commenced his post at the hospital. Daisy had a younger sister called Nira who had arrived from Israel and was also staying with her, so that it was fun for the three of us to be together. Nira was later to marry an American Rabbi who was also studying to be an accountant. They also settled in New York. Nira was a very bubbly and lovable character and was very outspoken in her conversation giving all and sundry gratuitous advice. She would tell someone who was eating ice cream to stop and think how many calories were in it and so managed to spoil their enjoyment. They would not be amused. She went on to have three lovely children, two of whom became doctors.

Gary found accommodation for us, and Jonathan and I took the train to Boston. It was a lovely experience in the train which was very clean and roomy. It had an area equipped for mothers with prams in which babies could stay, and mothers could be served with coffee and cookies. We joined Gary in an apartment near Harvard Square in Cambridge, Boston. There were a few English doctors and their wives in the neighbourhood with whom we became friendly. This was an exciting neighbourhood on the Charles River in the middle of Harvard University which was full of students, some of whom would baby sit for us.

I was happy in Boston. Everybody was friendly and helped me with settling in and looking after Jonathan. Our apartment was unfurnished but the hospital had a warehouse where doctors who had become more affluent with seniority, deposited old furniture which one could borrow. We selected several items and also bought a few pieces of furniture such as a playpen and a television. The playpen was to become Jonathan's little house. Sometimes he rattled the bars when there was music or something he liked on the television. When he was one year old I thought it was time to give him a taste of freedom as he was beginning to seem like a prisoner, so I let him loose. I thought that he would run around the flat but to my surprise he did not move away from the playpen, and if I took him to another room he would go back to the playpen. Later in life he told me that he was happy and secure behind bars! The nearby supermarket was much larger than I had ever seen before. Opposite our apartment we could see Adam's House, one of the ivy covered Harvard Colleges. Our finances were limited; I had $21 per week for food but nevertheless we managed to eat well. Gary's work involved long hours and in the winter when there was snow on the ground for several months he left whilst it was dark and returned in the dark. On those winter days I made sure that I would not become depressed in my loneliness. Jonathan and I made our own entertainment and remained happy.

We made friends both in the apartment block and with work colleagues of Gary's. I managed to entertain some single doctors who were working in Boston with Gary, but far from home. An English doctor ate with us regularly. He was great company and kept us amused with stories of his work and romances; his name was Tony Brown. His romances did not run smoothly. He was a very honest and generous person and falling in love was a serious matter to him. If he was let down he would be devastated. He was a very large man and it was upsetting to see him tearful. One of the senior members of his department advised him to lose himself in work. He came to see me and said that he was working all hours of the day and night and didn't think he could do any more. In my opinion, any girl who rejected him did not deserve him; that thought seemed to console him especially after a glass or two of wine. We remained friends for many years, meeting each other in the U.S.A. and England regularly until sadly, he passed away.

A Japanese doctor who was on a scholarship in the Anaesthetic department would visit us. Although I had little money I made stews and pasta dishes. After the first helping, I would offer our Japanese friend more and he would always accept. I would continue to give him more until I had none left. He would begin to look uncomfortable and I did not realise that it was impolite for him to refuse more food as it would be an insult to the host, this apparently being a Japanese custom. He later became a professor in Tokyo.

Joan Riley was an English teacher and lived in our block and was a good friend. She was an intelligent girl but always seemed to find the wrong man. I used to be upset for her as I thought she deserved better. We continued to be friends when we all returned to England but lost contact over time. I do hope she found happiness.

Mrs Day was also a good friend who lived in an apartment above us. She was an elderly lady who was rather lonely. She did not like to stop talking or leave our flat in a hurry. Before concluding a sentence she would interrupt herself by introducing a subsidiary sentence to explain a word or phrase she had just used. Her departure at the door could take up to one hour. She used to give me a lot of American recipes and she also loved our little boy, Jonathan, and sometimes baby sat. On one occasion, Mrs Day was downtown in a department store; she went to the toilet and hung her handbag on the hook on the door. Whilst she was sitting there she saw a hand come over the top of the door and remove her handbag which contained her door key and wallet. As soon as she could, she reported what had happened to the management. They took her phone number and address and she returned to her apartment; she gained entry with a key she had left with a neighbour. A short while later, her phone rang and she was told that her bag had been found in the store. She took a taxi to the store but when she got there she was told that nobody had called her. She returned home to find that her apartment had been ransacked. This was very upsetting and we tried to console her.

Gary had to work one month on nights. It was at this time that the "Boston strangler" was at large and I would barricade the door of our apartment at night.[8] The strangler used to target women who lived alone. He would pretend convincingly that he was a Priest on a mission of mercy helping the needy and particularly new immigrants as he was one himself. Most days there would be warnings where he might be and this was usually in the area where we were living. It was a frightening and unpleasant time for me. Eventually he was caught after we left Boston. In later years there was a film made about the strangler starring Tony Curtis.

During our time there the President of the U.S.A., John F. Kennedy was assassinated.[9] I can remember exactly what I was doing when the news flash came on T.V. It was lunch time and I always switched on the T.V. when I fed Jonathan. It was such a shock because one minute he was waving to the crowd in Texas and the next minute he was shot. America went into mourning for her young and popular President. Ideas abounded as to how this tragedy could have happened and even to this day conspiracy theories abound.

My cousin Myrna, who was studying medicine at the Hebrew University in Jerusalem, came to visit us for a vacation. We were very close as children, as we still are. Although we are thousands of miles apart, we still see each other as often as possible. I am older than her so I used to boss her around. I am also very fond of her sister, Judy, and brother, Yossi. I had a special relationship with their father, Sassoon, which I did not have with my father. While she was in Boston, Myrna went with Gary to the hospital to watch an open-heart operation for which he was giving the anaesthetic. She was very excited as she had never seen this sort of surgery before. She later continued her medical studies in Canada when Uncle Sassoon and his family emigrated to Montreal from Israel. This happened while we were still in Boston. We hired a car and drove to Montreal to visit him. We were accompanied by another anaesthetist who was acquainted with the route. It was autumn and the trees were colourful as we drove through New England. It was a beautiful sight, and we had an exciting reunion with Uncle and the family. Uncle and I had a long talk about my leaving Israel without his knowledge. I explained that I could not take a chance about letting him know of my departure because there was always the risk that he would not approve of my plans for safety reasons. To my surprise he assured me he would have supported me as he always knew I was capable of looking after myself. He told me that he was very pleased with all my achievements. We ended our discussion with a big hug which had never occurred with my parents. We visited Montreal on several more occasions in later years.

Our year in Boston soon came to an end. Gary had gained much experience but we were looking forward to seeing our family again and we flew back to England. I had very mixed emotions. We were now a family with a child, no home of our own to go back to and very little money. One thing was certain; we could both get jobs in a short time which was one of the good things about having a profession. We could have stayed in the United States if we had wished, but Gary preferred to return to England. I felt rather sad saying goodbye to America, my cousins and the friends that I had made, as well as the easy way of life. A friend of ours was driving to New York for a few days and offered to take me and Jonathan so that I could say farewell to my cousins there. We agreed not to say "Goodbye," but only to say, "See you soon," and we have managed to return to New York on many occasions.

FIFTEEN

Return to London

On our arrival in England, we went to live with my mother-in-law in North London and Gary and I both returned to the hospitals where we had previously worked. Jonathan had to be looked after by my mother-in-law while I worked, but I made sure not to do long shifts even though I knew Jonathan was well looked after. Gary was then appointed as a Registrar to a group of specialist hospitals in Central London. The commuting between home and work was long and tiring. The winter was cold and we did not have a car and Gary developed influenza and a chesty cough. He developed some severe asthmatic attacks and I found that the combination of work, bringing up Jonathan and worrying about Gary was stressful. My mother-in-law became very nervous when Gary was ill and I had the added burden of comforting her. I wished so much that I was back in the U.S.A. in my own place; emotionally I was at my lowest point. On Gary's recovery, life began to improve and the next step was that he entered the Department of Anaesthetics at Guy's Hospital, London. We moved into a flat in a purpose built block belonging to Guy's. I was very happy to arrive there. Although I was fond of my mother-in-law it was good to have my own place at last; for me it was a palace. There was no shortage of baby-sitters as the building was full of nurses and married doctors. The area in

Bermondsey was colourful but impoverished and the surroundings were reminiscent of the descriptions by Dickens of the poorer parts of London. There was a public house (pub) in our street where children would sit on the pavement outside in the summer until closing time when their parents would emerge to take them home. Gary, having obtained his Higher Degree, became a Senior Registrar. The Senior Registrar post was a rotating one. The first year was spent at Guy's Hospital in London, the second and third years were at the Brighton Hospitals, and the fourth year was back at Guy's, if a Consultant post had not been obtained by then. It was exciting to live in the centre of London. I am not a country girl and I enjoyed the hustle and bustle of the city. I became acquainted with many of the shop owners around Bermondsey. They were very friendly but London was proving to be expensive with our limited funds. There was a greengrocer nearby and I advised him to put his best fruit on display in the window, which he did. It was a very hot summer that year and the fruits ripened rapidly and when I went to buy them they were only half price. I did feel rather guilty about my advice to the owner.

Whilst living at Guy's I had my second child Sophia, who was born by Caesarean section, as had been the case for Jonathan. A colleague of Gary's, Ross Watkin, anaesthetised me. He and his wife Jackie were good friends and we still keep in touch. During 1967 when Sophia was born, we had saved enough money for us to travel to Israel to see my parents whom I had not seen since they had left England when I was getting married, almost six years previously, and now they were to meet their grandchildren. We would visit all of my family that I had not seen since I secretly left Israel. The four of us arrived in 1968 on a hot evening. Sophia was four months old and Jonathan was five years old. Our arrival was a very emotional occasion. Cousins, uncles and aunts came to the airport to greet us and we drove from house to house visiting relatives who were delighted to see me again. It was Gary's first visit to Israel and we spent every day for two weeks being taken to visit my relatives. My father was confined to a chair and my mother was doing well. She had obtained a job as a dressmaker working for a pleasant lady, and as time went by my mother became very friendly with her and her family. I was pleased that she enjoyed her work and was as cheerful as she was able to be. With her mental condition it was always good for her to be with people. My father spent most of his time reading or listening to the radio. My only wish at that time was to be able to help them financially. I was sad that I was unable to do so. In later years, I made sure that my mother was secure and I rewarded the people who had been kind to her. When I visited her I always took my two children with me to meet their grandmother and this seemed to bring joy to her.

Gary also had family in Jerusalem and we travelled by train to visit them. As we passed through the Judean Hills on the train from Tel Aviv we could hear shots as some fighting was still taking place. The train was full of young male and female soldiers, some lying on the luggage racks and singing Israeli songs. It was the first year after the six-day war of 1967 and the Independence Day celebrations took place the day after our arrival. There were parades and fly pasts.

We went to visit my cousin Yeheskel; he had a small apartment which he shared with his cousin Munera. Yeheskel never worked and some said he had won the lottery and lived off the interest which that generated. Although leading a simple life he liked to dress in the most fashionable clothes. He would wear a suit and tie over a smart shirt, and enjoyed strolling through the neighbourhood like this in the stifling heat of the summer in a Tel Aviv suburb. On our subsequent visits he would request materials such as mohair from England to have made into suits. We tried to converse in the Arabic we had used in our youth in Baghdad but Yeheskel was proud of his command of literary Arabic and accused me of using language which he called "street" Arabic. The story of Yeheskel and Munera is a sad one of love doomed for all time. As young adults the two cousins who had known each other since childhood were expected to be linked in matrimony, but she, Munera, rejected Yeheskel. In later years, after the deaths of their parents, they were obliged to share their accommodation and now Munera wanted to marry Yeheskel, if for no other reason than to legitimise their relationship before the community as they were living in the same dwelling. Now Yeheskel no longer wished to have a relationship with her as he wanted to show his resentment for her previous rejection of him. In their old age it was not a harmonious existence. Unfortunately, they never discovered the word "Love" even though they were searching for it.

My cousin Doris and her husband Morris were now living in Tel Aviv with their two children. They took us into the West Bank and we visited Nablus and nearby Mount Gerizim, the home of the small group of surviving Samaritans who live there. My cousin, Yeheskel, took the four of us to Ashkelon and so we saw a great deal, but the time to return to England came only too soon. Before we left, there was one more person I needed to see. It was my cousin Sabiha who had prevented me from obtaining a passport. In fact, she was very sheepish and apologised for the way she had mistrusted and treated me. She said that she was very pleased at the way that everything had turned out for me. I was not convinced of her sincerity.

The whole trip had turned out to be very emotional and mentally exhausting.

Our other vacations were spent with Gary doing locums in General Practice and Anaesthetics. In the summer we travelled to Caistor in Lincolnshire where Gary covered the practice of two doctors and we enjoyed the life in a small market town. We had a house-keeper who asked me each day what we wanted to eat and would then buy whatever we requested and cooked it for us. Her husband, who was the gardener in the large grounds of the house, would select the vegetables and fruit he grew. It was a very healthy and nutritious diet. About nine p.m. Gary and I would be presented with a tray of hot drinks and some nibbles. I felt like the lady of the manor in a period movie. We repeated this lovely experience on three occasions. The town was old fashioned and the people were very friendly and we will always have good memories of Caistor.

Our stay at Guy's was most enjoyable for me. Two Sisters in the hospital who lived in our block of flats would baby-sit for me regularly. One was a Sister Tutor and the other a Sister on the Maternity ward. Jonathan would insist that they read him a story in bed just as his mother did. We were able to go out in the evenings when Gary was not on duty. I would take Jonathan to Hyde Park where he would try to catch fish in the Serpentine, the lake in the middle of the park. He had a stick with a length of string attached and although he was very patient waiting for a fish to arrive, he caught nothing but weeds and pieces of discarded rubbish. People liked talking to him as he seemed so wise and charming for his age and he was also a good companion for me. I liked calling him Jon Jon but when he was naughty I called him Jonathan so that he knew that I was angry with him. The wives of some of Gary's colleagues would visit me at lunch times and various friends would call in for drinks in the evenings. The year passed quickly and the time came to move to Brighton. We were both apprehensive of this change and we were not sure what to expect as we both loved London. Before we moved, I went back to work for two nights a week at the West End Hospital for Nervous Diseases in Soho. It was good to be back again; I liked my work and got on well with the patients. When I arrived at night they would clap. I would bow back to them in appreciation and it was sad to leave when we had to move to Brighton.

SIXTEEN

Brighton

We drove to the South Coast where we were provided with an apartment opposite the Royal Sussex County Hospital. It was in a block of four apartments which were all occupied by doctors from the Anaesthetic Department and their wives, who were all nurses. We were welcomed by the Administrator of the Department and the other junior staff. Dr Rex Binning, who was the Chairman at that time, was very friendly and provided every help for us in settling in. He was a colourful character, charming and popular with the ladies, including me. His wife, Geraldine, was equally charming and they had two lovely children. They were very friendly with Sir Laurence Olivier and his wife Joan Plowright who lived in Brighton. Their children went to the same school as our children. Dr Binning entertained us in his home and we soon realised that Brighton was going to be a happy place in which to work. The doctors in the department were all friendly and had a busy social life with frequent "get-togethers" in restaurants in the town. The beach in Brighton was pebbled and an area was designed for children with a small pool encircled by sand. Jonathan started at the preparatory school for Brighton College. Gary was still doing locums abroad during his vacations as we were saving money for a deposit on a house. Gary's next arrangement for an anaesthetic locum was for a month in Sweden. It was an exciting adventure for us and the children. Despite all the travelling that we undertook over the years, our children seemed to adjust quickly to the new places and new faces, and I always tried to make some fun for them wherever we were.

Our children were now attending local schools.

Diana, Gary, Jonathan and Sophia

While Gary was away, I was shopping one day with my little daughter Sophia and had lots of parcels with me. I was running to catch the bus and bumped into a gentleman. My shopping scattered in all directions and I was almost in tears. The gentleman kept apologising and insisted on taking me home in his car which was a relief. I was speaking in Hebrew to Sophia and he seemed delighted and joined in as he spoke a little of the language himself. He had spent some time in Israel so we had much to talk about. For many years he had been living in California and was in Brighton to visit a sick uncle. The next day I received a big bunch of carnations. This caused some excitement amongst the other wives. It was a good story for some time and I found it amusing. We corresponded for a long while until he got married. I also nursed his uncle for short periods while he was living in Brighton recovering from a hip operation. He was a sweet old man who would send pocket money for the children. When he was feeling better he flew to Florida for some warmth to help his recovery. This was another goodbye that I did not enjoy.

Jonathan was now studying for his G.C.S.E. at Brighton College and he did very well in the examinations. Sophia was studying at the High School. In the late 1970s we travelled to Florida for a family holiday. Gary and I and the children loved this holiday and the following year we went again. We became aware that certain apartments in the hotel in which we stayed were being sold off as time-sharing properties where one could stay for one week each year. We decided to purchase two weeks and we stayed there for several years, and also exchanged those weeks for holiday resorts in the U.S.A. and Europe. The children loved their holidays in Florida and we befriended many people during these vacations. Jonathan was now working at school for his 'A' levels and hoping to achieve the requisite grades to study medicine, like his father, and it was during one of these holidays that he heard the results which were not sufficient to enter the medical school where he had been offered a place. At the time we were very upset, but in retrospect we were rather short sighted as we realised that Jonathan was not cut out to do medicine as he was, and always had been, interested in computing. We were due to visit some Caribbean Islands but he did not wish to continue the holiday as he had decided to return home and try to get a place at Imperial College to study computer science. I cannot say that I enjoyed the rest of my holiday without Jonathan. I kept worrying about him and wondered if he would achieve what he wanted. I made sure not to spoil the holiday for Gary and Sophia and I put on a brave front. We continued our holiday visiting the beautiful island of St. Martin and we then flew to Haiti. There we stayed in a hotel that had previously been the residence of Napoleon's sister and her husband General Leclerc. Napoleon had sent him there in order to restore the island to French rule following the revolutionary activities of the native General Toussaint l' Ouverture. This island had been ruled by a dictator and his son in recent years and the poverty was apparent wherever one went. The island had been popular with many authors including, Graham Greene whose book "The Comedians" had been filmed on the island. We travelled around in a taxi whilst it was raining and water appeared in the taxi up to our knees as we drove through flooded roads. The taxi driver explained that there was not a proper drainage system in the streets of Haiti. There was much corruption and little care for the welfare of the people. In addition, the police presence sent fear among the population. Our hotel room was set in the middle of the hotel's grounds and surrounded by trees. If you required service you had to ring a bell outside your room, whereupon scary faces appeared from behind the trees so we decided not to ring the bell. Within the room, lizards ran up the walls and bats would appear at night. Witchcraft was still prevalent on the island and the beat of the drums could be heard in the forests at night.

Jonathan had been on our minds all the time and we were relieved when he called to let us know that he had been offered a place at Imperial College. He sounded very happy and we were very pleased to hear this news. By this time I was glad to be heading for home, but not before I said goodbye to a little girl that we used to see regularly in the market. She would follow us wherever we went and became very attached to us. When we saw her sitting with her mother she ran to us as usual and we tried to explain in French that we were leaving. I gave her some pocket money and this was a tearful goodbye.

My mother continued to work at the dressmaker's shop in Israel. The owner and her family had become like a family to her. I would visit her every year and she came to stay with us frequently. I arranged for a bright young girl to bring her to us. After a few years of that arrangement my mother's sister became ill and passed away and my mother was no longer happy to stay in Israel. I thought that it was time for her to come and live with us in Brighton. She also thought it was a good idea especially as people who worked with her were insinuating that her own daughter, me, did not want her. This was very hurtful especially as some of our family also had that idea. It is intriguing how people draw their own conclusions without knowing the facts. We had previously encouraged her to stay with us but she did not want this. Now, however, she decided that she would like to leave and come to us. At the shop where she worked they began to help her to get ready for her departure. They even brought her suitcase to the shop in readiness for her leaving. Despite all this, they kept insinuating that no one was coming for her and it was all a big joke to them. We were making arrangements as quickly as possible. Gary took a week's leave from his work and offered to go and get her himself as a surprise. I thought it was a lovely idea as she would feel so proud in front of everyone. When Gary walked into the shop everyone looked up and started clapping. They must have felt guilty for teasing her. Gary told me later that my mother's face lit up, it must have been like a scene from the movie "An Officer and a Gentleman". I wish I had been there to see this. My mother did not speak English so I don't know how they communicated on the journey to England but I do know that they liked each other. I wish the same could have been said in respect of my mother and Gary's mother. The two ladies were not fond of each other. It was a blessing that they could not converse. For some reason they both insisted on sitting on the same settee, so, even as they sat side by side they carried on their dislike of each other in silence. It was rather sad. There was an amusing side to this as my mother sat at one end of the settee and took very little space as she was of slight build; she would point politely indicating what a large space she had left for Gary's mother as she was rather a large lady. I think this rather sly insinuation amused my mother as my mother-in-law was not pleased with the obvious reference to her size. I informed my mother that I was aware of what she was doing, but she claimed that she was innocent of any incorrect behaviour but welcomed sharing the settee and helping my mother-in-law to be comfortable. I am sure I detected a sly smile on her face. It gave me pleasure that my mother enjoyed watching old films on the television. I would have to tell her the story in advance and translate as the film progressed. She remembered some of the stars from the past and it was important for me that she did not get bored.

Apart from his clinical duties, Gary had to help in the training of the junior doctors. In this way we came to know these doctors well and I began to entertain them for dinners and parties where I cooked my pastas and stews for large numbers. Gary was involved in organising the equipment for the new Intensive Care Unit which was to be one of the earliest in the country. After about eighteen months in Brighton we were starting to think about returning to London. We would be sad to leave Brighton. I did my utmost to try and stay in Brighton and most of the doctors wanted us to do that. I also became friendly with some of the nurses who loved to baby sit for our children. One day I received a call from Doctor Binning who knew how much I wanted to stay in Brighton. He said that there was going to be a vacancy on the Consultant Staff because a senior lady anaesthetist had agreed to marry a millionaire she had met on a cruise and had given in her notice before she had even returned to dry land. She was not coming back to the hospital. He hoped that this would be a good opportunity for Gary. We were both very excited with this news. The post would soon be advertised in the British Medical Journal and although there would be no guarantees, Gary was the local candidate which might be advantageous. The Consultant Staff were encouraging. Having been short-listed, Gary went to the interview in London, as Brighton was part of the South East Region whose headquarters were in Croydon. After a nerve wracking day Gary was duly appointed as Consultant Anaesthetist to the Brighton Group of Hospitals. This meant that we would have to find new accommodation since our apartment was for junior staff only. I gave a party for the occasion, the drinks flowed freely and it proved difficult for some to cross the road back to the hospital where they lived. That remained a popular story for some time to come.

We purchased a house in Hove (sister town to Brighton) with the help of a large mortgage, and moved in with our few possessions. Entertaining was now much easier for me as I had ample space and a garden. Apart from routine anaesthetic sessions, Gary became Director of the new Intensive Care Unit. He had gained much experience in this field both in the United States and at Guy's, and he would spend many hours in this Unit. The wife of one of the juniors in the department was running a service for the local general practitioners in which she provided doctors to cover their practices for holidays and sickness doing surgeries, night emergencies and weekends. This included visits to patients and undertaking surgeries in their practices. When the time came for them to leave Brighton our friend handed the business over to me. As we knew a large number of junior doctors who were pleased to earn some extra money because their National Health Service (N.H.S.) salaries were low, I managed to recruit enough doctors to fill the demand which grew with time. I also managed to recruit Gary to do a few sessions for me. He made a good General Practitioner and became popular with the patients. This enterprise served as a useful introduction to the organisation involved in acting as an employment agency. It also gave me an opportunity to get to know the general practitioners and hospital doctors who worked in their off duty hours. The general practitioners were billed for the cover they received and the doctors who worked in the N.H.S. were then paid. The general practitioners were happy to have had the relief and the doctors who performed the locum duties were happy to receive the money. Overall, junior doctors in the N.H.S. were poorly paid and were very happy to work for extra remuneration.

Many of the locums would come round to our home to pick up their cheques rather than waiting for the post to arrive as they needed the money as soon as possible. They would come to our house and make it a social occasion; they all seemed to like visiting us which was pleasant but rather tiring. I also became an agency "agony aunt".

We became friendly with a couple living opposite us. Ian Thomson was a cricketer who had been a fast bowler for Sussex and England but was now a teacher. His wife Eileen, who had been a secretary, was later to become my personal assistant and the book-keeper for my business. They had two daughters, the youngest named Tracy was about nine years old at the time, and she became friendly with my daughter Sophia. They played together but later Sophia was abandoned in favour of her brother Jonathan as Tracy discovered that boys were more interesting. Eileen and I not only worked together, but were best friends. She was the best colleague anyone could have. We never argued and I respected her opinion in all manner of decisions. When my mother came to live with us, Eileen and her husband used to stay in our house in order to look after her when we went on holidays. I will always appreciate her friendship. We had a gardener who was an Operation Department Assistant (O.D.A.) helping the anaesthetists. He was full of good stories about the hospital personnel, and after I had given him toasted sandwiches for his break, he rewarded me by his stories becoming more exotic and elaborate.

After a year or two in our house in Hove we began to look for a house with more space. Although the G.P. Locum business did not bring in much money, Gary was now earning more and was editing and writing a book entitled "Intensive Care" He was doing this in collaboration with colleagues at the hospital who represented different specialities. The book, incidentally, was one of the first of its kind and was a great success and went into a second edition. This was a busy time for us as we were both working, Gary was writing and I was looking after the children. I am a great believer in organisation, and following a routine made everything fall into place. My theory is that if children are left to their own devices, life can become confusing and they are happier knowing what is expected of them and what to do next. It was interesting that if I lapsed now and again in my routine they were the ones to complain.

Although we liked our house and the neighbours with whom we had become friendly, we began to look for a house near to the sea. At that time my cousin Yossi, who was a medical student at the Magill University in Montreal, came to England for a few months to gain experience in orthopaedic surgery. We finally found another property and I fell in love with it immediately. It was in a crescent in Hove opening onto the sea front with views of the sea from the main bedroom window. The house had been empty for some time and had been vandalised, but it still had the style and space of a special residence. Apart from the five bedrooms, dressing room and four bathrooms, there was a very large conservatory which proved ideal for entertaining. The house had previously been owned by a solicitor who worked for show business personalities, actors and celebrities and many of them had been entertained there. These included Liberace, Rock Hudson, and Laurence Olivier who lived in Brighton, Sophie Tucker and The Beatles. In fact, Ringo Starr spent his first honeymoon in this house. It took some time to restore the interior to its former state, but we carried on as best we could during the restoration process.

SEVENTEEN

Sweden

In 1970, we travelled to a town in the north of Sweden called Solefteå where Gary deputised for the anaesthetist in charge of the department in a large modern hospital. We took our car, crossing the sea by ferry and then driving to the north. I enjoyed seeing a good deal of the countryside as we stopped at several towns, resorts on the coast, and lakes. As it was summertime, it stayed light most of the time, and the children would play late into the night – whereas in winter it stayed dark for most of the day. We stayed in the house belonging to the anaesthetist who was on holiday. His name was Paolo and he was an Italian; his wife was an English nurse called Gloria, they had two children and were a charming family. Gloria was most helpful and briefed me about shopping etc. We discovered the cost of living was very high in Sweden and we had to be careful with our money. We stayed friends for a long time and they now live in Sicily.

There was one off-licence store in Solefteå whose opening hours were restricted. A Salvation Army man would stand near the door to warn people of the evils of drink. We would try to sneak into the shop unobserved but exiting with the incriminating evidence was more difficult. Before we were reprimanded we gestured that it was too late. On subsequent visits he would say, "Too late," with a smile before we said anything. I thought he had received the message. One day with tongue in cheek I asked him if he would like to join us for just one small drink. I saw a little smile on his face and I had the feeling that he was reluctant when he said, "No thanks," and he added that his brother was the Mayor of the town and would not be amused. It would not be pleasant to suffer his anger! On that note, we bid each other a cheery goodbye.

Whilst we were there, a curious thing happened. In Brighton we had known a doctor who frequently arrived at our flat opposite the hospital and would stay talking to me even when I was busy with the children and Gary was working. His visits were long and although I was busy I did not like to offend him. We had thought that we would not see him again by the time that we returned from Sweden as his post at the hospital was due to finish. One evening as we were eating some fish caught from the local river, Gary, after a long silence at the table very slowly and very carefully made the announcement that although he did not know how our friend had located us at such a remote place, he had arrived in the town and intended to visit us that evening. I thought at first it was a joke, but it was not, and trying to say something in my shocked state I swallowed a large fish bone that was in my mouth. I thought I was choking and had to be rushed to the hospital to have it removed. It was like a tale of the unexpected.[10] The following year when Gary was going to do another locum in Sweden, I decided not to go as it was too long a journey for the children and we would be able to save more money. I knew it was going to be hard for Gary surrounded by caring Swedish, blonde nurses, but I thought I would let him suffer!

EIGHTEEN

South Coast Locums

It was whilst we were entertaining some junior doctors in the mid-1970s the subject of providing locums for hospital doctors arose. In order to understand the background to the agency that I was about to open, I must outline the situation at that time for N.H.S. junior doctors working in hospitals. The number of junior positions in each speciality was limited, so this meant that the junior doctors had to work long hours. This resulted in very good experience for them but sometimes tiredness negated the advantages of experience. The N.H.S. could not readily cope with the absence of junior doctors due to sickness, vacations, compassionate leave and any other unexpected event. To obtain a locum through the routine channels was very difficult for short term needs. An advertisement in the British Medical Journal (B.M.J.) took two or three weeks, replies needed to be assessed, short lists prepared, interviews arranged and references checked which meant that even for permanent appointments the process was difficult, but for short term arrangements there was no chance of success. This meant that existing junior staff, already overburdened, had to do the work of absentees. The most difficult time for covering the medical duties was at the end of their six months' appointments in July and January. At this time there was often a gap in the changeover and it was here that the medical agency could help to avoid chaos. The increased expenditure for the N.H.S. was well worth the improvement in the continuity of patient care. At the same time, the doctors who performed these locums were receiving payments which they badly needed.

It was with this background in mind that we were discussing the problem of one of the junior paediatric doctors who had booked a holiday some time in advance, informed his department and had the dates confirmed. One of his colleagues had fallen ill suddenly and he had been informed that he would not be able to take his holiday because of the necessity to help cover the emergency duties. His consultants had said that there would not be a chance of finding a locum who was sufficiently experienced to perform these duties. In this case, the junior paediatrician had a friend who had completed an equivalent post in another hospital and was now between appointments. In view of my experience with the G.P. Locum agency, he suggested that I inform the administrator in charge of personnel at the Children's Hospital that I knew of an experienced paediatric Senior House Officer available if she needed one and I could provide the names and contacts of the Consultants that he had worked for in this field. I agreed to do this and the next day I telephoned the administrator concerned and after some discussion with the Consultants, the doctor was invited to come immediately to the Children's Hospital to meet them and take up the position. This was the start of the agency which I named South Coast Locums. There was a similar agency in existence in London, but mine was certainly one of the first in the South of England. Our new house had some spare rooms so I decided to use one of them as my office. The room I decided on had much clutter in it so I asked my daughter and her friend, who were both nine years old, to clear it for me for a reward. They worked very hard and the end result was very impressive. I paid them 50p each which wasn't very generous of me, and they did not seem very pleased. I explained that we had not negotiated a price but they would have further rewards when I started to make a profit; that's business! To this day my daughter reminds me of that incident and how I turned into a hard business woman overnight, and that I still owe her compensation for being underpaid. Is she trying to make me feel guilty? I think so.

The news soon spread amongst the hospital administrators and the local hospital junior doctors. The Brighton Hospitals were also linked with two London Teaching Hospitals which meant that their doctors who rotated with Brighton for training appointments also heard about my agency. I sent my tariffs to hospital personnel administrators in the South of England and in a short while I sent a Senior Surgical Registrar from a London Teaching Hospital, who was shortly to become a Consultant, to cover a Registrar post in a South Coast Hospital. Soon after he arrived, a serious emergency (a ruptured Aortic Aneurysm) was admitted. He successfully operated performing surgery that only a specialist Consultant Vascular Surgeon usually performed. This achievement was impressive for the Consultants and helped to establish my reputation as a reliable locum agency. It soon became necessary to seek help with the administration of the agency. I called on Eileen, who had been my neighbour, and she began to keep the books and arranged cover for the various requests when I was not available. All this we did from my home so that I was always around for my children.

In order to successfully fill the posts which were requested, there were two important matters to arrange. In the first place, experience in the correct speciality, and secondly, if possible more seniority in that field than the doctor whose post had to be filled. Gary helped me in these decisions until I became familiar with all these aspects although, as a trained nurse, I understood the various problems. Doctors who came on my list of available personnel had to have a curriculum vitae (C.V.) outlining their experience, certificates of their qualifications and insurance cover by one of the medical insurance agencies. References from previous appointments were also required. These were all passed on to the personnel departments at the hospitals. Doctors from Australia, New Zealand and South Africa, as well as India and Pakistan came to work for my agency and proved to be very successful. A common practice for Australian and New Zealand doctors was to purchase a camper van in England and then tour Great Britain and Europe working as locum doctors to pay for their visit. When their time came for their return home, they would sell their camper vans to other doctors who would arrive in England and repeat the cycle. Most hospitals provided accommodation for their locums who might stay for several weeks.

In one of the local hospitals there were four Irish doctors whose appointments were ending. They were approached by the administration to extend their appointments. They answered that they could not as they all had grandparents who were not well and it was important for them to return home quickly as they were very fond of them. These doctors came and registered with me knowing that I would get a call from the hospital with a request to fill four vacancies, which I did the same day. These were locums for three weeks until new replacements arrived. The doctors were desperate and I called the hospital and gave their names. There was a long silence at the other end of the 'phone and when the administrator found her voice she said, "They are our doctors who said they could not stay on because of the illness of their grandparents." I said apparently their grandparents are now recovered so they registered with me. I could imagine the lady shaking her head as she told me not to worry about their details as she had them already. She also added that it was odd how the extra money they would receive from the agency cured their grandparents' illnesses quickly.

My relationships with both the junior doctors and the hospital administrators were excellent. My services were needed by both and the N.H.S. benefited from this service. Many of the administrators and doctors became my friends over the years. Indian doctors would introduce me to their new brides, Australian and New Zealand doctors were fond of visiting our house by the sea front and discussing their lives and work over drinks. Some of the hospital administrators became personal friends. Payments from the hospital finance departments could be slow sometimes so when any of the doctors needed money badly, and this happened often, I would pay them on completion of their work and before I had received money from the hospital. I think this was one of the reasons so many of the doctors remained loyal to me. I was always being given advice by people who thought I should be more businesslike and make fixed times for payments. However, I could never work with such rules, especially as some of the doctors made it clear that they needed the money which they had earned and I understood and saw no point in only paying on certain days. This way we developed a certain bond and I made sure to let them know how much I appreciated them. My job depended on them and we needed each other. When a doctor contacted me, I never opened the conversation by asking what I could do for them. I did not find that a friendly start to a conversation. I did not feel that I needed to have any power in doing my work.

One of my secretaries, a large and powerful woman, would on occasion, visit a Finance Department when payments were long overdue. Although she did not threaten them directly, she always seemed to come back with a cheque. I noticed that whenever she went on her mission to request a large amount of money that was overdue, she took her walking stick with her which she normally hardly ever used. I also found out she used a mild threat by saying politely that if the hospital was short of funds we would help them by withdrawing the doctors that were working for them at the moment as there was a great demand for them elsewhere. On hearing that, they would quickly produce the cheque that was about to be posted. On that note, she would leave by announcing that she looked forward to seeing them if they had any difficulties in posting a cheque. After that we did not have any further delays in payment from that hospital. Somebody I knew who worked in the Finance Department wondered where I found such a lady who was more like a hit-man than a secretary. Eileen, who kept our books meticulously, was always congratulated by the Inland Revenue inspectors who would visit us annually. It had always been a pleasure to receive visitors to my house, but a visit from two of Her Majesty's tax men was not so welcome. As the door bell rang, it did not sound the usual noise and the two faces that appeared as the door opened resembled passport photographs with no trace of a smile. Eileen and I accompanied by the accountant were on our best behaviour and dressed sombrely for the occasion, but the young secretaries who were not included in the meetings floated around dressed in shorter skirts than usual and managed discreetly to cause a flicker of distraction, especially when it was time to serve the tea and cakes. The tension diminished and the atmosphere became as relaxed as one could hope for with such visitors. After bidding them goodbye and closing the door, we all sighed with relief and promised ourselves a drink. The one thing I was reprimanded about was the large amount of expenses recorded in entertaining the doctors.

As my business expanded and awareness of the possibility of getting help became more widespread, I needed more help and I employed some part time ladies to help with different shifts and making it easier for Eileen who was so valuable to me. I had many different characters who worked at the agency; there was one who was always slimming but kept forgetting that she was supposed to be on a diet when it came to coffee and cakes. Another who was newlywed, would arrive crying on Friday mornings because her husband had done the cooking on Thursday night and she thought that it meant he did not like her cooking. One secretary tried seriously to teach her dog to spy on her husband when he took the dog for a walk. She was convinced that her husband was having an affair when he was out with the dog. I asked how did the dog let her know, and she explained that when they returned from their walk, if the dog put his head down and kept shaking it, he was unfriendly towards her husband which means that her husband had talked to a woman that evening. If the dog came home looking happy and wagging his tail it meant that her husband was not having any illicit conversations. Another secretary liked to flirt with the doctors. She gave some of them her home telephone number and told me it was for fun and that her husband trusted her. Little did she know that there was a microphone under the telephone table – so much for the trusting husband! He contacted her while she was working and told her he had heard her conversation. She had to flee home quickly before he arrived to create a scene. This lady was quite good at her job and a likeable character but she seemed to suffer from several ailments which seemed to manifest themselves whenever a doctor was around. She made it clear that their opinion would be appreciated on that particular day and it was usually necessary for her to get partially undressed. I had to exert my authority to stop these requests and not let the doctors go through such unnecessary ordeals.

I covered more locations and supplied hospitals around the British Isles, even as far as providing locums to a hospital in Benbecula, near Stornoway in the Outer Hebrides. The hospital had at one time been provided with a medical officer from the R.A.F. However, when they could no longer supply medical help, the administrator requested a locum cover from my agency. The doctors had to fly and travel by ferry to reach the hospital. They had to be on duty for twenty-four hours at a time as they were the only doctors there, so that meant that they were getting very good remuneration. Being on duty every day for twenty-four hours on this island did not mean that the doctor was necessarily overworked. It was a very quiet hospital and major surgical cases needing operation were transferred to the mainland. Nonetheless, the hospital was obliged to provide twenty-four-hour medical cover. One of these doctors was very well qualified and also charming; his name was Balapa. He was from India and became very popular. He was so well liked that he stayed almost three years and was accompanied by his wife. Unfortunately, she could not conceive so he decided to take a week's vacation in order to visit Jerusalem. He had read much about the town and especially about the Western (Wailing) Wall and how one could pray there and write a wish on a small piece of paper and insert it into a crack between the stones. He asked me many questions about Israel as if it was a magic land. I was not able to answer all his questions as I did not have enough knowledge. When they returned his wife was soon found to be pregnant. I had a phone call from the hospital informing me that Mr Balapa had changed his name to Moses. We were all amused, but I never knew why he did so. It may be that the Prophet Moses had something to do with his wife conceiving! It is just a thought! Needless to say I was very pleased for the lady. Regardless of how she obtained her wish, it was an amusing story with a happy ending.

There were also some sad stories connected with some of the doctors who worked through the agency. Three female doctors, who all died, were regular visitors to our house, two of them being sisters. These two came from a large and poor family. They were very clever and had worked hard at their studies and had achieved their ambitions and those of their parents. Their siblings had likewise succeeded by hard work. This showed that given the determination and potential to make something of yourself, regardless of your background and with some support from your family, much could be achieved. Sadly, they were not happy in their personal life. One was deeply in love with the wrong person who let her down; she could not take the upset and took her own life which was a great waste. I will never pass judgement on people's feelings, but it is hard to understand how one can take a precious life especially for a doctor whose mission it is to save lives as well as causing long lasting grief on those who are left behind. Her sister, who was a very bubbly person, was devastated by this loss and I assume that due to this grief she took a fatal overdose resulting in a terrible tragedy for that family, it certainly was for me. I had a call from the mother saying that her husband had gone into decline refusing to accept what had happened. She was devastated and trying to search for answers as to what had happened. Had she failed her daughters by not getting involved in their personal lives? She felt that their actions were a reflection on their parents. She found it very unpleasant to see the notifications in the local newspapers and presently was unable to leave the house. I did my best to console her and reassured her that the girls who had become good friends of mine had nothing but praise for their parents and the happy and loving home they had shared with all their siblings. By the end of our conversation, I was also in need of help and support.

There were also two male doctors who died in car crashes. I telephoned the family of one of them to offer my condolences; his grandfather answered, he was crying and saying it was not fair as he was ninety and still alive while his beloved grandson was gone. It was too sad to continue this conversation. I was choking with my own tears by this time. It came to my knowledge later that one of the doctors who died had become very fond of a nurse. I understood that they were very much in love; he was Australian and she was expecting his baby. His parents were very supportive unlike her parents. She left for Australia and I understood from her friends that she was made very welcome by the family and is happily living there with her baby son.

There were of course many funny stories connected with my work. One day, I asked one of the doctors who worked for me to do a long weekend in psychiatry for which he was well qualified. He said that he could not do it because his brother-in-law was coming for a visit from India. He did not think he could cope with his wife's wrath if he worked. I had to think fast as to how I could persuade him to work because this was a speciality of mine, so I asked him if he liked his brother-in-law. He paused for a while and I quickly said, "I have a feeling you don't." "Not really," he said. I said, "Well, there is your answer, to lose a lot of money for someone you don't like, it's a great shame especially with the new school term starting and all the things needed for the children, three of them." I had to remind him of the number. He paused sighing and said, "You are a very persuasive lady and I will do the job." He even stayed beyond the weekend to avoid the family. I think King Solomon would have been proud of me. The doctor later told me that his wife did not cook his favourite curry for three months – what a punishment!

Some doctors who worked for the agency were of special interest. There was a Formula 1 racing driver who was later to become a commentator for the sport; there was a champion squash player, a sculptor and relatives of famous people. A few of the doctors were well-known "Don Juans". These always proved to be a problem. They were good looking and charming and the nurses became besotted with them. One of these doctors kept telling me how the nurses found him irresistible but that he knew how to handle them. His diary must have been full with dates. On one occasion he mistakenly made dates with two nurses on the same evening. Luckily they were in two different hospitals. He rang me frantically and asked me to make excuses for him. I managed to find a good excuse, although I felt sorry about this and I never sent him to either of these hospitals again. Some of the nurses would telephone me to enquire where some doctors were working and I had to avoid revealing their whereabouts. One of the doctors who worked for the agency was very good looking and full of charm. He was an excellent cricketer and most of his spare time when he was not working for the agency was spent playing cricket. It was by working for the agency that he was able to combine medical duties with his cricket matches. One of the nurses fell madly in love with him after their first date. She refused to accept his inability to spend more time with her. She would telephone me on numerous occasions and I had to try and explain that his commitment to his work and his cricket took up most of his time and that there was no other girl involved. This girl asked one of the hospital porters to watch him playing cricket and report to her any suspicious liaisons. The porter fell asleep half way through the match, so I was told by the doctor who recognised him there, and I think that was the end of the love story.

I was often asked to provide locum cover for psychiatric hospitals in the south, and many strange things happened in them. One of the doctors had a patient who came into his office with a knife in his hand. He asked the doctor, "Who should I kill, you who locked me up with all the mentally sick people, my mother-in-law who called me crazy, or the incompetent chef who starved the patients by cooking inedible dishes and who should never have been called chef? I see no reason to be kept here indefinitely so that you can keep such an easy job." The patient had a manic look in his eyes and the doctor had to think quickly. He asked the patient to sit down and think about it over a drink as it was a very difficult question to answer. As he was sitting down, the doctor mixed a sedative in orange juice which he gave to the patient and that is how the danger was averted. The doctor also related how on one occasion a visitor was locked in the ward which had tight security. He called the nurse to let him out but the nurse, who was new, refused to let him out. He told her not to delay him as he had a train to catch, her reply was, "Haven't we all," as she still believed that he was a patient.

My house was always open to all the doctors and their families. I always needed lots of food and drinks in the house as some of the doctors had nowhere to go when they were off-duty. Occasionally some of the doctors would stay at our house. My parties were getting larger now, especially as we had a big house and garden, and our children loved helping at these parties. It was a hectic life and very tiring. My job involved long hours and sometimes went on well into the night if there were emergency staffing problems at the hospitals. Working from home was never easy but luckily my staff, and especially my friend Eileen, were always very helpful. The good thing about working from home was that I was always available for the children. There was a girl called Trish (Patricia) who was working for a General Practice Group. She came to work with me and soon adopted us as her own family as she had lost both her parents. She had a sister called Wendy, and a good friend called Sue who had a great sense of humour, and they all came to our house at evenings and weekends. Trish became friendly with several of the New Zealand doctors and their wives, who introduced her to a friend. They fell in love, became engaged and I gave them a big party. Her fiancé left for home and Trish joined him in New Zealand to make a happy ending. I enjoyed "matchmaking" even though it was hard to say goodbye. Trish came back three years later with Evan, her husband, and their little girl, Hannah, and we had a good time together. Trish has now settled in Invercargill, New Zealand and Hannah is now at University studying architecture.

My mother, who was living with us in Brighton, started to get bored and agitated. It was rather upsetting for me as I thought she would be happy here in England. However, this was not so and we seemed like two strangers. She had always suffered with depression for as long as I could remember. She could not speak English and did not understand what was happening around her. She missed her work where she was proud to earn her own money so she became increasingly unhappy. I thought of an idea and I asked her if she would like to make dresses for little children. I would sell them and we could share the profits. Her face lit up. I was so pleased and I went and bought her a sewing kit, materials and an old hand operated Singer sewing machine; she was back in business. She started to make the dresses and I would pretend to sell them. I would give her money for this and take my commission! It made her content but of course it was all a game as no one was going to buy the kind of dresses that she made. The charity shop was full of my mother's old fashioned designer dresses. It made the perfect therapy for her. I took this lovely idea from a book called "The Woman in White".[11]

Whilst running South Coast Locums, I befriended a lovely family called the Wilsons. I met them through one of the daughters, Caroline, who was a personnel manager at one of the hospitals where I supplied locum doctors. The Wilsons had a beautiful house with large grounds in the countryside in West Sussex. Part of the house was used for guests. My daughter and I spent many happy weekends with them. Mrs Wilson senior, who I called Ma, was a delightful lady and an excellent cook, and she used her skills to prepare frozen meals and hampers which I would buy for my own use and for gifts.

We wanted our daughter, Sophia, to go to the Brighton and Hove High School for Girls. We were informed that it was difficult to get admission to this school. However, we entered her for the test at the age of five and she was successful, but after that I was not so popular with some of the mothers whose daughters did not succeed. I find this kind of attitude does not bring harmony or happiness in the community.

I wasn't always the successful matchmaker. Sometimes I failed, as when I introduced two doctors who were Irish, neglecting the fact that they were from opposite sides of the Border, (north and south). I left them alone in the garden with a drink in order that they got to know each other. They certainly did with a heated political debate, far removed from friendship, let alone a love match. All I could do to cool the situation was to give them another drink and direct the conversation to another subject. There was another time when I thought that I had the perfect match. A close friend of ours who we considered very charming was visiting from the U.S.A. He was originally Welsh and we had met him in the U.S.A. whilst Gary was working there. I had an attractive lady doctor who was working for the agency at that time who also came from Wales. I thought that this match could not go wrong and I arranged some snacks and drinks for them. When the lady arrived I was about to introduce them but they eyed each other in shocked silence and then informed me together that they needed no introductions as they had known each other since they were children and there were obviously no pleasant memories. They had been neighbours but not neighbourly as they had always competed in their careers. It was a relief when that party came to an end.

The personnel officers of many hospitals were very happy with the help in staffing that I was providing. The work was very hard but my experience as a nurse and my husband being a hospital doctor helped in finding the appropriate locum doctors. We had two telephone lines and they were constantly busy. Working from home meant that there were no breaks such as lunch times. My daughter would complain about the hours that I was working. She was not very happy at school, which was an all girls' school, where girls could form groups and exclude others. She had some friends who enjoyed coming to our house. The education at the school was excellent but Sophia was determined not to send her own children to an all girls' school if, and when, the time came. She did well in her 'A' levels which consisted of science subjects, although she was also competent at art and French. Sophia went on to study Dentistry at University College, London, like her grandfather who was also a dental surgeon. My husband, Gary, has had dental treatment at different times from both his father and his daughter. Sophia enjoyed her time at University and made many friends. Some of them would visit us in Brighton and I would provide them with a lavish buffet. They were always very surprised that I could do this at short notice and would call me "Mary Poppins". The credit for this lovely meal belonged to Ma Wilson. I would smile sweetly and thank them for their compliments and they would reward me with a beautiful bunch of flowers the next day. Sophia also spent some time in Israel visiting my mother, before my mother came to live in England. After qualification, she started working in a dental practice in Brighton.

The relationship between Gary and my mother was amusing. They communicated with scattered words and signs so their conversations were short and sweet. They would watch snooker together and bet on the likely winner. My mother was an expert in making Turkish coffee and I would sometimes visit Sophia in London for a night or two knowing that they would be happy in each other's company. My mother's diet was small and simple. It consisted of cottage cheese, hard boiled eggs and small pieces of cold chicken. She would boil several eggs at a time and put them in a corner of the kitchen. Gary would sometimes play a game with her by replacing the eggs with tomatoes. She would become very puzzled at how this had happened but she would finally see the joke.

While I was running the agency, I had a frightening experience. It was towards the end of the day and I was alone upstairs in my office. The front door was mostly unlocked as

171

there were so many doctors arriving at the house at all times. I heard footsteps downstairs and was going down to investigate. At the middle of the stairs I came face to face with a burglar. He looked rather pathetic and not at all menacing. I asked him who he was, and could I help him? He pointed a finger at me and said I was very naughty for leaving my door open. I could not believe I was having this conversation so calmly with a burglar. I thanked him for his advice, and he said that was all right, but could he have a couple of Aspirins for his headache. I apologised for not having any. He said, "I thought it was a doctor's house as it said so on the front door and you don't even have an Aspirin!" He shook his head, and I said I would be grateful if he would leave so that I could lock the door and return to my work. He turned around and went out of the door whilst I was still standing on the stairs. I sighed with unbelievable relief and thought to myself that I will wake up now and find that this had been a dream. He did not take any money and, strangely, I felt sorry for him, so I ran out to give him some money but he had disappeared. Now when I tell this story to people they find it hard to believe. I have even lost the friendship of one of my cousins, as he refused to believe my story and considered it an insult to his intelligence. He told me that I did not seem to understand his intellectual abilities and a story like mine is not one that he can accept. He told me that I had not forgotten to tell imaginative stories and if I wanted to do this, could I please try them on other people. I find this cousin very sure of his own importance and I think that is why he was not very popular. I must admit it was a bizarre story, but it did happen and to this day I cannot understand how I got away safely. When I told my neighbour, who happened to be outside, what I was trying to do she could not believe what she heard. Was I insane running after a burglar to give him money instead of calling the police? I think she enjoyed telling the street about my mental state and I received some strange stares from some of my neighbours. It always puzzles me how people make judgements without knowing all the details. I was not given a chance to explain. I did not have a case to present to the police because I was not attacked, nothing was stolen or disturbed in the house and the man walked away peacefully, even without an Aspirin. I could not have given much of a description of him. He had a sling around his neck but his arm was not in it. He said that he came in to warn me about my open door so what would my complaint be?

One of the nursing sisters, with whom we were friendly, was travelling to Egypt to visit her son who was working there for an international company. Gary and the children encouraged me to join her, and my staff assured me that they would be able to cope. On the day of my departure I left home very early in the morning without waking anyone. On the way to the airport an uneasy feeling suddenly struck me. It was the thought of not seeing the family or saying goodbye. I revealed my thoughts to my companion and she said to dismiss such thoughts as I would be back safely. I had always wanted to visit Egypt with all its fascinating history. When I was a little girl in Baghdad I would watch Egyptian movies and I was familiar with their stars. The movie industry in Egypt was very popular in the Middle East and I preferred the dialect and melodious sounds to those of other countries. To me, Egypt was a miniature Hollywood. Previously, it had not been possible for me to travel there because of the strained relationship between Egypt and Israel, but now because of the more relaxed situation between the two countries it was a good opportunity to accompany my friend. I must explain that my travelling companion enjoyed non-stop talking! She was a lovely, kind lady who was very fond of animals, as I am. At Heathrow Airport, my friend and I boarded the 'plane and took our seats. There was a lady sitting near the window and my friend sat next to her, and I was by the aisle. Even before the 'plane took off, the constant chatter started and it was not even interrupted by the noise of the jet engines. By now, the lady who was sitting quietly by the window became included in the chatter, not by choice, although she was not responding as she was trying to read. I bought my friend a few whiskies in the hope that she would become sleepy, but this had the opposite effect and the chatter continued. After almost an hour of this non-stop torture, I was very sorry for the lady by the window who began to get restless and agitated. She suddenly got up, excused herself, and that was the only time I had heard her voice. My friend presumed that she had gone to the washroom and when she did not return for a long time, she began to wonder why she was away for so long, but I could see that she had changed her seat as the 'plane was not full. I was not surprised, but my friend was! On arrival at Cairo Airport we parted. She was met by her son and I went to my hotel. My room was on the twentieth floor so I had a good view over the city. It was a very pleasant hotel and the next morning I enquired about going on some tours. I joined a group of people, many of whom were from England. Visiting the museums in Egypt is a great experience, especially seeing the pyramids and the Sphinx illuminated at night. I continued my tour with the group by visiting the pyramids and having camel rides, and everybody taking photographs. It was exciting having to crawl inside the pyramids where some of the Pharaohs were buried. Afterwards, the tour guide gave us a lecture on how the pyramids were built by the people as a token of love for their Pharaohs. I put my hand up to correct him. My explanation was based on the facts that the Hebrew people built them with hard work and sweat and not with love as they were slaves. Some of them could have been my ancestors. Suddenly I was the centre of attention. The crowd looked at me with curiosity and irritation. The guide was taken aback by my outburst and he asked me what proof had I got for this statement. My reply was that these facts were in the film "The Ten Commandments" and my witness was Charlton Heston who played Moses in the film. I do not think the guide was amused and neither was the rest of the group. I think my presence was causing discomfort within the group, although my dispute had been fun for me. The guide offered to have a private discussion about it, which I declined. I sensed that he did not take kindly to my refusal of a discussion. For me, it was a joke and I was expecting to get a laugh, however to him, it was a question of honour as I had tarnished the Pharaohs' name.

After that visit I was becoming bored and restless with this particular tour so I decided to travel alone and visit certain places on my list prepared by Gary. I took a chance and chose a taxi man that seemed reliable and he did not object to me leaving his name and taxi number at the hotel reception, who informed me that he had a good reputation. We toured around for two days visiting old synagogues and Coptic churches, and then I took a boat trip on the Nile seeing all the movie stars' houses. I was rather alarmed when I boarded the boat and realised I was the only passenger. The taxi driver noticed my hesitation and explained that he would accompany me and that the boatman was a friend of his. The taxi driver took me home to have tea with his family, and my choice of driver turned out to be an enjoyable experience. I also wandered on my own on the streets near the hotel in order to get the feel of everyday life in Cairo. It was helpful that I was able to speak the language, and an asset that I had watched so many Egyptian films as Egyptian Arabic is spoken in a special dialect. I also visited the beautiful opera house which at that time was playing Aida in Arabic but I did not have time to see it.

Towards the end of my stay in Cairo, I was enjoying a relaxing bath in the evening when suddenly the water started shaking and things started to fall off the shelves. I rushed out of the bath into the living room and things were shaking there as well, and then the whole building began to shake. I was on the twentieth floor of the hotel and people were running in the corridors. I did not know what was happening or what to do. I stayed in my room as I did not think it was wise to leave. Out of the window I could see all the cars at a standstill and small buildings below were in ruins. It was an earthquake, and it was a weird and frightening feeling being alone and miles from home. My main worry was about our children losing their mother. After what felt like a very long time, the shaking ceased and the hotel remained undamaged. I had been holding a photograph of my family and I had been crying, but now I told myself that my time was not up yet. My thoughts went back to the morning I left without saying goodbye or seeing them but then I remembered how they all knew how much I loved them. At midnight, when I looked out of the window, the traffic had started to move and by the early hours the telephone lines had been reconnected. I called home to let the family know that I was safe as I knew it would be on the news. Gary answered the telephone in a very sleepy voice. He informed me that he was rooting for me as if I was a football player involved in a match. I was not amused by his phrase, and having enquired about the children and sent them my love I ended the conversation. I never managed to visit my friend and her family in Egypt with all the chaos and disturbance of the earthquake, and we returned home on different dates. It certainly was a memorable visit.

On my return home, I made sure to ask my mother-in-law not to use the word "Enjoy" when we were heading for holidays in future. Every time that she wished us to enjoy a holiday something unusual of an unpleasant nature happened. My mother-in-law did not like us going away. I suppose she felt insecure and lonely without us. So it became a joke that she never said, "Enjoy your holidays". She informed me that she would use a different phrase in future. I suggested she said, "See you soon with a nice present for me". She seemed pleased with this especially the sound of a present.

I used to donate my house for Jewish charitable functions as it was ideal for entertaining large numbers. Fate played a big part in one of these functions. The Jewish community in Brighton entertained a group of Israeli soldiers for a holiday by the seaside in England and my house was chosen for a welcoming party. Shlomi was one of the soldiers and became very friendly with my daughter Sophia. He came back to England for a few visits to be with her and each time they grew closer and I realised that my daughter was falling in love. I thought that this might be happening too quickly, but she reminded me that this happens all the time in the movies and that I should know better than dismissing this in real life. I should be happy that all the romantic movies that I had been watching all these years were actually taking place here and now. I did not point out that life was not a movie because I realised that I was being over protective of my daughter, perhaps because I had never experienced much protection myself. I was happy to see them together, especially as we liked Shlomi and his family when we met them on our next visit to Israel. Shlomi's mother is an excellent cook and her dining table is usually full of all kinds of tasty dishes. His father is a great host. He fled from Bulgaria as a teenager during the Second World War. He also has a charming brother and sister. My adventurous daughter decided to try to obtain a dental qualification in Israel. Gary, who by now had retired, wanted to learn Modern Hebrew so we decided to rent an apartment with a beautiful sea view for one year in Tel Aviv. I stayed in Brighton working but I visited them frequently. We got to know Shlomi's family who were very friendly. Sophia and Shlomi's relationship was getting stronger, and in the meantime in England my son, Jonathan, had found a girlfriend and wanted to get married. We had a lovely wedding for them in Bournemouth by the sea. In time, Jonathan opened his own computer software business which is still operating successfully. He and his wife, Joanna, have four delightful children and I love them very much. The year 1995 was a busy one as Sophie and Shlomi decided to get married in Israel. Family and friends came from all over the world to the wedding, and after that we all returned to England. I am a very lucky grandmother as Sophia and Shlomi had two lovely daughters. I helped to look after the children as babies because both their parents were working. It was a pleasure for me to do this, just as it was with all my other grandchildren.

I had been running the general practitioner service and then South Coast Locums for hospital doctors for almost thirty years and now things began to change. New locum agencies started up and the National Health Service was economising on the employment of locums as its financial position was worsening. Some departments in hospitals were finding that they could save money by employing additional full-time staff in order to cover holidays and illnesses rather than using agency doctors. Pressure was applied to administrators to do their utmost to find doctors to work long periods as locums at N.H.S. rates, and the arrival of the European Union regulations meant that doctors from abroad could be employed to work in the United Kingdom at the standard rates. I realised that the time was coming to gradually run down the business. I had always had many extremely friendly and loyal doctors whom I was privileged to know. Some of them would find their own employment and do the locums through my agency. There had always been a special bond between me and some of the doctors, as well as the staff that worked with me. I tried not to let it upset me. I had been devoted to my work and was proud to have done it well. This time was quite emotional for me with all of the memories. I had made so many friends and my relationships had been more than business but based on these friendships with such interesting people. Although I had always been a good talker, I was also a very good listener. I remember one occasion when I was giving a party for the doctors who had worked with the agency, together with their wives or partners; I was so absorbed with getting everything prepared that I had left no time to purchase a new dress. All of a sudden, one of the doctors' wives who knew me well arrived with a big box saying that she knew I would not be spending time on myself so she brought this dress for me. Inside was a summery white dress with a lovely white flower for my hair. This time my appearance in the mirror was much improved. I now understood what it felt like to be Cinderella with a Fairy Godmother. I had a passing dream that my father would have approved of all I had done.

NINETEEN

Epilogue

By now Jonathan and Sophia had left home, and without the offices of South Coast Locums our house was too big for us. We had to think about moving. My mother-in-law lived in a flat in Brighton and we didn't wish to move too far away. Sophia had settled in Portsmouth where she and her husband were working, and Jonathan was in Bournemouth. After a long deliberation we decided to move to Portsmouth, it was not far from Brighton and I reassured my mother-in-law that we would visit her every weekend and take her everything she needed. We kept that promise to the end. I loved Portsmouth from the moment we moved there, I have always loved to be near a port with its ships and sailors. Gary insists that he is a sailor because he was a doctor on a P & O liner for a few months which made him a fully fledged sailor and the reason I fell for him! He still manages to find audiences to reminisce on his days at sea even though it has been more than fifty years since he sailed and he was no Sinbad.

I had a strange feeling about Portsmouth; that I lived there many years ago and that I was a chambermaid who worked for a kind lady who gave me time off to see my sailor boyfriend. We married and had many children who were all boys and all became sailors, and we lived happily ever after! My grandchildren love that story. I must admit that I liked the story myself and enjoyed telling it, and as time went by I added more to it in order to make it more colourful.

My granddaughter, Naeve, was born shortly after we moved to Portsmouth. She was premature and quite ill and we were all relieved when she came home.

My dentist was in Gosport which is a pleasant ten minute ferry ride from Portsmouth. Sophia worked in the practice there. On my numerous visits to the dentist I observed a man and a woman who arrived in separate cars, got on the ferry and affectionately kissed, then started to work on papers that were inside an attaché case. They continued to hug each other whilst continuing to work on the papers. On one of these occasions a smartly dressed lady boarded the ferry and sat quietly at the back. As the ferry docked she jumped up, ran to the couple and grabbed their attaché case and threw it overboard. As soon as the ferry tied up, she jumped off and shouted at the couple, "Swim for it!" I presumed she was a wronged wife (the fury of a scorned woman!). It always puzzled me why men and women have to hide their infidelity if they are truly in love with each other. Why don't they come clean and face the consequences? Is it cowardliness or selfishness or is it that they don't want to hurt the people involved? However, deceiving and cheating is not honourable and it is better to make a definite decision, although I know that is easier said than done. There is certainly a thrill in leading a double life but I am no judge on that issue.

While we were living in Portsmouth, I had a call from my cousins Myrna and Judy from Canada telling me that thirty members of my family, headed by my Uncle Sassoon, were going on a cruise to Alaska. I was delighted that we would be able to join the family as it would be a special event. We all met in Vancouver where Uncle knew a relative who lived there and contacted her about our arrival. We had to stay for two nights in a hotel before embarking on the Holland America Line ship. When we arrived at our hotel there were parcels awaiting every member of the family containing snacks and water, and an invitation to our relative's house for a welcoming party. Limousines were awaiting us in the evening and took us to her home which had spectacular harbour views. We were pampered with a wonderful buffet and champagne which was an unexpected surprise. There was another surprise to follow when the time came to pay the bill on our departure from the hotel. We were told that it had been dealt with already by our lady cousin and the hotel manager. It was overwhelming for me to have such a lovely gesture from a cousin that I hardly knew. Our mothers were first cousins and she was older than me. I tried to remember when I visited her in their large house where I could play hide-and-seek and where once I fell asleep whilst hiding and no one could find me, except the dog who detected my hiding place. On the cruise we were joined by her and her daughter who was aged about twenty. I became very friendly with the daughter and we shared our love of the cinema by going to see a film every day on the ship. Other activities were not so successful, especially bingo where I caused considerable confusion. I did not seem to be able to understand the rules. My cousins did not wish to be associated with me and told me that I was too intelligent for such a game! Certainly the cinema was a safer environment for me. The cruise to Alaska was very unusual. We sailed between British Columbia and the islands off the coast (the Inside Passage) and then along the Alaskan coast. We called in at several ports in Alaska and I went ashore to each of them. On the cruise, Gary never failed to attract a gathering to describe the story of how I managed to trick him into marrying me so that I could obtain British citizenship. Each time he told the story it became longer, especially about how he tried to resist. On the strength of that story he managed to get several free cocktails. It was a splendid reunion for the whole family and long to be remembered. It was the last occasion I would be with my uncle for a long while. At the end of the voyage we disembarked in Vancouver, and Gary and I bid the family farewell and flew to San Francisco where we had a friend who we had known in Tel Aviv. Her name was Madelon and she was a tourist guide. She took time off to show us the city and its sights, and then took us for a tour of the Californian vineyards. Unfortunately, we lost touch after that pleasant time together. It is sad that one cannot stay in contact with all the friendly people that one meets in life but, at least, one has the memories. San Francisco is an enchanting city which you don't wish to leave in a hurry. Our friend took us to a dinner theatre called 'Beach Blanket Babylon' where the actors impersonate current celebrities.

Learning to drive had its fair share of funny moments; I was never good at following instructions or manoeuvring the car. The neighbours' curtains used to twitch every time I was collected by the driving instructor. He was a good instructor and never gave up on me. It was quite a different tale with my first instructor; after the first two lessons I noticed that my usually calm instructor seemed to become very nervous which had a bad effect on me. I was driving a manual car and suddenly I shot into fourth gear and we had to stop with both of us shaken. We had a long discussion about the importance of concentration whilst driving. We spent the remainder of the lesson driving slowly and safely but as we reached home with all the neighbours watching I managed to mount the pavement! The following lesson included a three-point turn; I don't know how but I kept turning as if I was on a carousel and unable to stop. The instructor asked me if I wished to continue with the lesson and I said, "Yes please." I was determined to show my skills at the next lesson but in my eagerness at the emergency stop I pressed the foot brake so hard that we almost shot through the air. Well that did it, the instructor took over and we drove home in silence. He admitted defeat and told me that in his profession he could not continue working with shattered nerves. He also reminded me that he had a wife and two children to think about. It sounded like a Greek tragedy when he told me that I should abandon the idea of driving. I did not argue, that was not in my nature to give up driving and we said our goodbyes politely. I started as a beginner with a new instructor and he was not of a nervous disposition. The day I passed my test was not good news for the neighbours. Most of them moved their cars from the street into their garages. I did not blame them and I must admit I surprised myself by passing the test on only my second try.

I have never had much of a sense of direction. On one occasion I was searching for an address in Hove where I was due to have a special X-Ray. A gentleman saw me looking rather lost and offered to help me when I said I was looking for a clinic. He seemed to know where it was and guided me gently to a building and departed in haste. When entering the grounds I realised that this was a psychiatric clinic and was amused to think that I must have seemed to be in need of such an establishment and I wondered what the psychiatrist would have made of that.

My daughter obtained a dental post in the town of Bournemouth working for the Council and moved there near to her brother. We also decided to move to Bournemouth. We were happy to all be living in the same town, but I did have some regrets about leaving Portsmouth. Bournemouth is a lovely seaside resort where I had spent my honeymoon.

Although Sophia was enjoying her work as a children's dentist, there was little chance of improvement in her career prospects. Although she was happy living close to us, she had to think about her future. She was next offered a post of Senior Paediatric Dental Officer for the Borough of Portsmouth and decided to return there with her family; her husband also finding work in that city. I began thinking about returning to Portsmouth in order to be able to help Sophia with her children whilst both their parents were working. I think one grows attached to a place that reminds one of happy times. Also, my two lovely grandchildren would like the idea of having me nearby and I was also popular with their friends! There was, however, a problem in that my son and his wife with their four children also wanted me and their grandfather to stay nearby.

When my father passed away in Israel, I was in England with two small children. I could not afford to travel there for his funeral. I knew my mother would be devastated. Apparently he was holding a conversation with her whilst shaving when he had a fatal heart attack. For a woman like her it must have been a terrifying experience. I wished I could have comforted her, but I saw her not very long after and it was not easy for either of us. On hearing of my father's death I had many memories and mixed feelings. I wanted badly to cry but tears just would not come. About one thing I was pleased, and that was that he saw his grandchildren before he died. There were so many things that I would have wanted to say to him. Was his behaviour due to the fact that he had been sent abroad to boarding school when he was young which resulted in a lack of emotion? I wanted to thank him for loving my mother and for being tolerant with me when I threw the occasional tantrum. I wanted to tell him that I could have loved him if he had only allowed me.

My mother passed away in Brighton after living with us for five years. Sadly, I think she wanted to depart from this world. She was never any trouble to us. I was very sad not to have been able to make her happy, but I do know she was happiest when her grandchildren, Jonathan and Sophia, were around. They managed to communicate sufficiently to let her know how much they loved her. She never really settled in England but she never complained and so I never knew what she was thinking whilst she sat through those long days. I worked from the room where she sat because I knew that she liked company and became distressed if she was left alone for too long. In order to keep her mind active, I would make her tell me stories of films she had seen in the past. The sight of our cat, Tom, reminded her of our cat Minnie in Baghdad and used to trigger a depression. She was pleased when I told her that Tom would be banned from entering the room. Poor Tom could not understand why he was no longer welcome in his favourite room. After her death, I tried to think what we had in common but I could not. She used to give the staff at South Coast Locums small amounts of money from what she had supposedly earned from her dressmaking. She had always been generous; that much I knew about her. I also found a little money in her purse which was my inheritance! I would have liked her to have been buried next to my father in Israel but it was not to be. As my parents were first cousins they were very close and in love with each other. I did not think that I was included in that love. In their own way they thought I had everything that I wanted or needed, and they forgot about the emotional side altogether. I was a puzzle to them. Being an only child I would have been very lonely if it wasn't for all of my cousins, aunts and uncles. I spent most of my young days at one house or another, reading my books and watching movies at the cinema. I made my own happiness and that was good enough for me. I did admit to myself that I put a brave front on being tough and having a "couldn't care less" attitude. Deep down it did hurt, especially when I saw how other children loved to climb on their father's lap and get a loving hug and kiss. I never attempted to do that. I did not find my father's lap inviting. Looking back on it, I think it was sad for both of us. Having to love and trust people, I conditioned myself to tread gently in my relationships in case of rejection. However, life works in mysterious ways, and the kind of people with whom I came in contact, touched my life with love and kindness, caring for me although I was a stranger. From this, I have learned how to treat people with similar love to that which I received and I will always be grateful to all those who helped me on my way through life.

There is a saying that, "While you are busy making plans, life is busy making plans for you". I was beginning to get some abdominal pains which I kept trying to attribute to different causes. Trying to ignore them was to be a big mistake as they continued for some considerable time. Eventually, I visited my General Practitioner who felt a lump and referred me immediately to a surgeon who said he would need to operate immediately. I now realised that the problem was serious, but there were no tears. The scan showed that I had cancer. I did not question "Why me?", as I thought that there were so many people in the same position. I knew from my nursing experience that Consultants felt unhappy delivering such news to their patients. I broke the silence by announcing that I had to go and cool a bottle of champagne. I knew it was rather an unusual thing to say, but it brought relief to the tension in the room. I went home and enjoyed a glass of champagne. The next day I went to the movies, and the day after I had my operation. The operation revealed a cancer of the colon and the surgeon removed the right half of my colon. The fact that the diagnosis was made at an early stage of the cancer helped greatly in my recovery. The Consultant who operated on me became a friend because of our shared love of the movies. I did my best not to dwell on my condition but let each day go by as I recovered. I read a lot in hospital which I preferred to having many visitors. In the post-operative period I did my best not to feel sorry for myself and say "Why me?" There is nothing special about me and that is the way I faced the problem, "Why not me?" It was decided that I should not have radiotherapy and chemotherapy but would need frequent check-ups. My wish is to see my grandchildren grow up. God has been kind to me and I am grateful I have been spared so far. I shall never take the small things that we do every day for granted. As I got better I wanted to make the most of my blessings. I get a lot of pleasure if I can contribute to making people happy, especially children. I always keep something tucked away to give to a child. It is a great feeling to see the smiles on their faces. I developed a special trick to play on children if I was in a sweet shop at the same time. Sometimes children would be counting their money to see if they had enough to buy the sweets they desired. Occasionally they would say that they did not have enough. I would drop some coins on the floor and they would hurry and pick them up and hand them politely to me. I would refuse to accept them saying that I was superstitious and believe that I would have bad luck if I took them. They would accept the coins with thanks and seemed to be happy to have met such a crazy old lady. I must admit I gained more pleasure from incidents like that than the children themselves. It gave me a good feeling and, maybe, I was a crazy old lady.

I continued to have further problems with my health associated with my previous surgery, and some new illnesses, but I tried to never let them interfere with my way of life. I went on to have two more major operations. After one of my check-ups, as I was cheerfully waiting for the results, my kind Consultant walked into the room without his usual smile. He did not stay standing up in order to make a quick announcement but sat down silently for a few seconds, which was not a good sign. To help him out I asked him if the cancer had returned. He had a very puzzled expression on his face and shook his head with a "No" without looking at me. He explained gently that he thought he had seen the shadow of a new cancer which was not related to the original one. This was rather unusual and he would have to operate without delay. I could see that it was very painful for him to give me this news. I must admit it came as a shock to me. I managed to break the gloom by saying that I did not like second-hand cancers and would sooner have a brand new one. I don't know if he appreciated my joke but it did bring a smile to his face, although it wasn't what I wanted to hear. My operation was successful and it was not easy to find the right words to express my gratitude. I was determined to get my strength back and at length it was wonderful to be able to do all the things I enjoyed, especially to be strong enough to be with my grandchildren whose favourite outings are to the cinema. I have tried to continue with my everyday tasks, going out and travelling, and I always try to see any good new movies. I continue to tease people and invent silly stories for amusement. My favourite sayings to the grandchildren are about how amazed I am each day when I look in the mirror and see how I am getting prettier by the day and I hope that they have noticed this too! They do not say anything but I am faced with silence and sniggers from all six of them. I then tell them in a serious fashion that I cannot wait for tomorrow. They all turn to look at me enquiring what is happening tomorrow. With a smile, I explain that I will be prettier tomorrow than today! With that announcement, six exasperated faces look at me with puzzlement and groan, "Oh Grandma!"

After two years of enjoying life, I began to have abdominal pains for which I was prescribed pain killers but they were not helpful. The pains became agonizing and not like those of my previous illnesses. Gary had to call an emergency ambulance that night and I had no recollection of what was happening, apart from the excruciating pain. When I arrived at the hospital I saw my Consultant's face in front of me and I thought I was hallucinating. However, it seems he was on duty and was working late. He did all the necessary investigations and operated on me immediately. As I was awakening he explained in simple terms that my condition had nothing to do with my previous cancers but was a perforated duodenal ulcer with peritonitis which I knew, as a nurse, could be very serious if not operated on in time. He reminded me that he was running out of DVDs to watch. I drifted off with a weak smile as I wasn't dreaming after all.

In my fifty-five years in England, the happiness and success that has come my way has certainly outweighed any unfortunate events that happened to me. Adopting England as home for me and my family was an excellent choice. I had no problem mixing with people and never faced any hostility or rejection, and I was always met with warmth and friendship. I would like to consider my life as a big movie, part drama and part comedy. To love and be loved has been the best part of it. The people who touched my life will be the part that will stay with me. To have been spared in spite of my health problems is like winning the biggest prize ever. I am now very happy at this stage in my life to be able to relax a little and let people think for me and advise me, which my grandchildren enjoy doing. I would like to conclude by saying that I shall continue to live my life to the full as long as I am able and permitted to do so.

Diana and her six grandchildren

NOTES

[1] Kings II, 24 (11-15).

[2] At a time of conflict between the British and the Iraqi government of the day, and influenced by pro-Nazi propaganda against the Jews, up to 200 Iraqi Jews were massacred in what was called the Farhud.

[3] Alliance schools were present throughout the Middle East. They were founded by French Jews to help the emancipation of Jews and to fight Anti-Semitism.

[4] On 29th November 1947, the United Nations General Assembly voted for the partition of Palestine into separate Jewish and Arab states. There were 33 votes in favour of the resolution, 13 against and 10 abstentions. France, United States and the Soviet Union voted for, China and the United Kingdom abstained. Fighting immediately erupted between Jews and Arabs in Palestine and this was followed by disturbances in Baghdad.

[5] On 14th May 1948, the British withdrew from their mandate in Palestine and David Ben Gurion announced the foundation of the State of Israel. Immediately five Arab nations, Egypt, Iraq, Syria, Jordan and Lebanon attacked the new State and the War of Independence commenced.

[6] 'The Samphire Gatherers', J. Rowe.

[7] Sinai Campaign: In 1949, following the War of Independence, Israel and Egypt signed an agreement to allow navigation to pass into the Red Sea through the Straits of Tiran so that Israeli shipping could reach Africa and the Far East. Fedayeen attacks, Egyptian rearmament and the blocking of the Straits of Tiran by Egypt for Israeli vessels, left Israel with little choice. At this time, Egypt had taken control of the Suez Canal from Britain, and both Britain and France saw this as a threat to their passage to the East and Africa which were trade routes and routes for their oil supplies.

Israel now saw the dangers of the new alliance between Egypt and Syria and later with Jordan. The Fedayeen attacks were becoming more frequent and the three nations i.e. Israel, Great Britain and France launched an attack on Egypt to restore the free passage of their ships through the Suez Canal and the Gulf of Aquaba into the Red Sea. After some very difficult and complicated battles, Israel succeeded in opening the Straits of Tiran whilst French and British Forces were attacking the Egyptian defences around the Suez Canal.

[8] Thirteen women were strangled with nylon stockings in and around Boston over a period of two years.

[9] Friday, 22nd November 1963, in Dallas, Texas.

[10] 'Tales of the Unexpected', by Roald Dahl.

[11] 'The Woman in White', Wilkie Collins, published in 1860.